teach®
yourself

html:
publishing on the world wide web

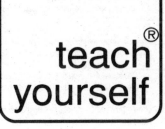

html:
publishing on the world wide web
third edition
mac bride

The **teach yourself** series does exactly what it says, and it works. For over 60 years, more than 40 million people have learnt over 750 subjects the **teach yourself** way, with impressive results.

be where you want to be
with **teach yourself**

For UK orders: please contact Bookpoint Ltd., 130 Milton Park, Abingdon, Oxon OX14 4SB.
Telephone: +44 (0)/1235 827720. Fax: +44 (0)/1235 400454. Lines are open 09.00–18.00, Monday
to Saturday, with a 24-hour message answering service. You can also order through our website
www.madaboutbooks.com.

For USA order enquiries: please contact McGraw-Hill Customer Services, PO Box 545, Blacklick,
OH 43004-0545, USA. Telephone: 1-800-722-4726. Fax: 1-614-755-5645.

For Canada order enquiries: please contact McGraw-Hill Ryerson Ltd., 300 Water St, Whitby,
Ontario L1N 9B6, Canada. Telephone: 905 430 5000. Fax: 905 430 5020.

Long renowned as the authoritative source for self-guided learning – with more than 30 million
copies sold worldwide – the *Teach Yourself* series includes over 300 titles in the fields of languages,
crafts, hobbies, business, computing and education.

British Library Cataloguing in Publication Data
A catalogue record for this title is available from The British Library.

Library of Congress Catalog Card Number: On file.

First published in UK 2003 by Hodder Headline Plc., 338 Euston Road, London, NW1 3BH.

First published in US 2003 by Contemporary Books, A Division of The McGraw-Hill Companies,
1 Prudential Plaza, 130 East Randolph Street, Chicago, Illinois 60601 USA.

The 'Teach Yourself' name and logo are registered trade marks of Hodder & Stoughton Ltd.

Copyright © 1996, 1998, 2003 Mac Bride

Typeset by MacDesign, Southampton
Printed in Great Britain for Hodder & Stoughton Educational, a division of Hodder Headline Plc, 338
Euston Road, London NW1 3BH by Cox & Wyman Ltd., Reading, Berkshire.

Impression number   10 9 8 7 6 5 4 3 2 1

Year   2007 2006 2005 2004 2003

contents

acknowledgements

Level 9 Software – for Ingrid Bottomlow and scenes from the Dribble Valley;

Total Connectivity Providers – for the provision of Web space, and all-the-year-round good service;

Named and unnamed contributors to the World Wide Web – for the screens I have captured, and the help and inspiration I have gleaned.

preface

I'll let you into a secret – *HTML (HyperText Markup Language) is simple*. Its vocabulary contains not much over 100 words, and its syntax is clear and logical. You can master enough HTML in a few hours to be able to create a basic Web page, and enough in only a few days to create far more complex ones. And it doesn't get much harder as you get further into it – you can get some very impressive effects with only the simplest code. Having said that, don't expect to be able to knock up a brilliant Web page in a few minutes. Good pages need a lot of thought put into their design, and a lot of time put into their implementation.

I have written this book mainly for home users who want to develop their own home pages, and for small businesses who would like to use the Web to advertise their products and services. It won't show you how to sell over the Web – that raises a host of legal and security issues that could not be fitted into these 220 pages.

This third edition has been extended to cover some of the new tags, and more importantly, style sheets that were introduced with HTML 4.0. I have also taken the opportunity to pick up some issues raised by readers of the first and second editions. Keep the feedback coming!

mailto:macbride@tcp.co.uk

http://homepages.tcp.co.uk/~macbride/tybooks

Autumn 2002

1
home pages

In this unit you will learn

- what HTML is about
- what a home page is
- how some people use
  their Web pages
- how to start planning your
  home page

1.1 HTML

HTML stands for HyperText Markup Language, and is the means by which Web pages are created and linked together. It developed from SGML (Standardized General Markup Language), and if you want to know any more about SGML, look on the Web at:

http://www.ncrel.org/~rtilmann/htmltools.html

This is a practical book, not a history book!

HTML is based on the use of tags. These are key words or phrases, enclosed in <angle brackets>, which describe how text and graphics are to be displayed, and which create links between different documents or parts of the same document. It is HTML's ability to handle links that makes the Web possible. The World Wide Web is essentially an ever-expanding set of interlinked HTML documents, and a Web browser is essentially a tool that can display these documents and follow up the links embedded in them.

In its first few years of the Web, HTML and browsers were under almost constant development – largely fuelled by the fierce competition between Netscape Navigator and Microsoft's Internet Explorer. This put Web page builders into a quandry. If they used features from the latest version of HTML in their pages, people viewing with older browsers would not be able to enjoy them. If you wanted everyone to be able to see your work, you had to keep it simple.

It's different now. HTML reached version 4.0 in 1998 and hasn't changed since. Every browser produced since then is able to handle all HTML 4.0 features, and 95% of people surfing the Web are using one of those newer browsers (mainly Internet Explorer 4.0 or 5.0). All of which means that you can take advantage of all that HTML now has to offer, knowing that your visitors will be able to enjoy it to the full.

1.2 What is a home page?

A 'home page' may refer to a simple one-page document belonging to an individual user, or to the point of entry into a huge site run by a multinational corporation. It may fit into a single screen, or may be so long that it fills 10 or 20 screens. It may consist of a single text file, or may have dozens of graphics, video and sound clips and other items embedded in it.

If you want to have a home page, it must be stored on a computer that other users can access. For big businesses, this means a machine that has been set up to allow two-way traffic; for individuals and smaller businesses, this means on their Internet service provider's machine. Most providers now offer free Web storage space to their personal members, and cheap space to their business users.

Your Web space

Check that your Internet service provider can offer you Web space. If they do not offer this service, change your provider now! And if you are shopping around, check how much space they will let you use free – some are significantly more generous than others. You may not have great ambitions as a Web publisher, but it's always good not to have to worry too much about limitations.

Personal home pages

So here you are, with Web space at your disposal, a desire for world-wide publicity, and two questions on your lips. What do I put on my home page? How do I do it? Both are rather large questions. I'll tackle the first one now, then take the rest of the book over the second.

1.3 What goes on a home page?

There are two aspects to this. What message are you trying to get across? What mixture of text, graphics, forms, tables and links to other files and pages will best achieve that aim?

The message

If you are running a business, the obvious use for your home page is advertising, and perhaps marketing your products and

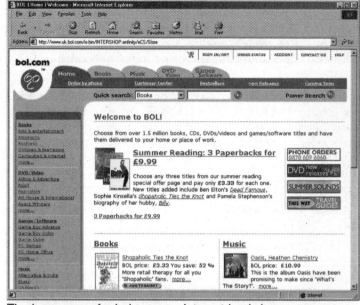

The home page for bol.com, an Internet bookshop.

A well-designed and effective home page for a club. The links on the left act as a 'Contents' list for the site.

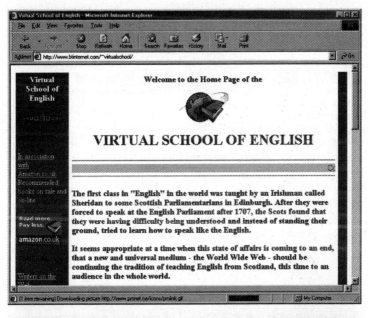

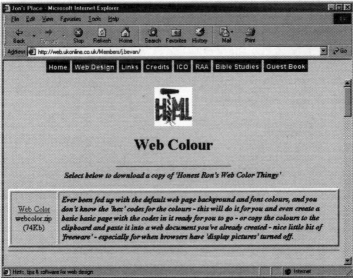

Two examples of home pages created by readers of earlier editions of this book, just to show where it can lead!

services. (Telling people about your products is straightforward, selling them over the Internet raises problems that are not tackled in this book.)

If you are the secretary or publicist for a club or society, the home page can be used to inform members – and prospective members – about its activities. It can also be used to gather feedback from members.

If you have a particular hobby or interest that you would like to share with others, you could turn your page into an information centre for that topic. If you are a fan of a star, a group, a writer or a TV show, set up a fanzine on your page. You do not have to be an expert to do this – just an enthusiast. Spend time researching the Internet and gathering together links to information and other resources. Make your page a prime jumping-off point for your subject, let everyone know that it is there and you will earn the appreciation – and perhaps the friendship – of fellow enthusiasts from around the world.

If you are a poet, musician, writer, artist or photographer, you can use your home page as a showcase for your works. (I don't think it is worth putting a novel or symphony on your page, as I can't see many people bothering to wait while it downloads.)

The one thing that is not a very good idea, is to use your home page solely to tell the world about yourself. Unless you are a celebrity, very few people will be interested in you. Sorry to break this news to you, but it is as well to know before you start to design your page.

The content

Text

Text is good. Text travels quickly over the Internet. And it doesn't have to look boring. You have lots of control over the size of the characters, and of the colour, placing and alignment of text.

Text is also easy to handle. You can lay out a page of neatly formatted text, with several levels of headings and ruled lines between sections, using only a limited set of very simple tags. With a little effort and a couple more tags, you can create bulleted or numbered lists of items. These aspects of text are all covered in Chapters 2 and 6.

If you are feeling adventurous, you can move on from lines of text, to text in tables. These can be a very attractive way to display organized information, though they are rather fiddly to set up – every part of the heading, every row and every item in the table needs its own tag!

We will leave tables until Chapter 8.

Graphics

They say 'a picture is worth a thousand words'. If you think in terms of downloading time, it would be better to say 'a picture takes as long as several thousand words'. The picture on the right (380 × 600 pixels), stored as a JPG file – the most compact format – takes 20Kb, which is enough for over 1,200 words – or about 8 full screens of text.

Depending upon the baud rate of your modem and the amount of traffic to a site, it takes anything from 5 to 25 seconds to download this much data.

If you are going to include graphics in your page, they must be either (a) worth seeing, or (b) small. People can get very irritated if they have to wait 2 or 3 minutes, only to find that they have downloaded an out-of-focus picture of your pet rabbit, or your firm's boring logo.

You will see how to add graphics in Chapter 3.

Some people include *multimedia* clips in their home pages, though the arguments about quality and download time apply to these, even more than they do to still graphics. You don't get many seconds of video in a megabyte, and it can take longer to download an audio clip than to listen to it! All service providers set limits to your Web storage space, and a few video or audio clips could push you up against – or beyond – the limits of your free space. Having said that, if you want to share pictures of junior's first steps with your friends and relatives in Australia, it's easily done through your home page – and they will think that it is worth the wait.

Multimedia clips are covered in Chapter 4.

Counters are a neat idea, and fairly easy to implement. Add one to record the number of visitors to your site. It is an effective way to assess how much interest your page is generating.

Cool links

No home page is complete without links to other pages – direct your visitors to your favourite sites, or to the good stuff that you have found on the Web. They will appreciate the links – with so many millions of pages on the Web, any pointers towards the best

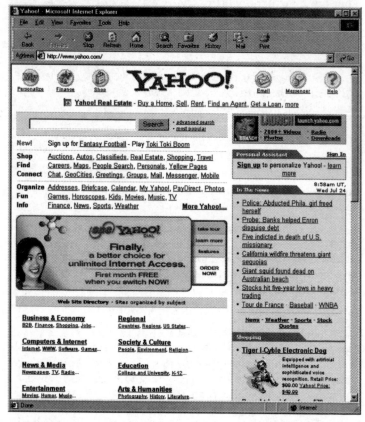

Get enough good links and perhaps you could take on Yahoo! Well, perhaps not, but it's worth knowing that Yahoo! started as the home page of two students. Some good things have come from a bright idea, a deal of hard work and a home page.

are always useful. Some people's home pages consist of little but links, and these pages can be highly valued by other users.

You will see how to create links in Chapter 4.

Frames

With **frames** you can divide a page into separate areas, each of which can display a different file and be changed independently. They can improve the look and the usability of your page, but involve a number of complexities. We'll leave those until Chapter 9.

Forms

If you want to get feedback from your home page, the best way is to use a form. This consists of a set of slots into which your visitors can write their names and addresses, or whatever other information you seek. If you are running a business, a form could collect details from potential customers. If you run your page as a fan club or enthusiasts' information centre, a form can provide a simple means for fellow enthusiasts to contact you.

This page has been divided into three frames – one for a title, one for a contents list and one to display material.

As a form is only a set of tags, with a little text, it adds little to the size or download time of a page, however, it does require the active involvement of your access provider. They must run software to collect data submitted by your visitors and pass it on to you. Most providers do this, but if feedback is going to be important to you, check that yours does – now.

We will look at forms in Chapter 7.

Image maps and applets

Image maps – larger pictures with several links embedded within them – are increasingly used to act as 'Contents' lists at the top page of sites. Image maps are not hard to create, as you will see in Chapter 10.

Java applets are small programs that can be embedded into pages, to be downloaded and run within your visitors' browsers. There are several sites on the World Wide Web where you can pick up ready-made applets to slot into your own pages. When you have got your pages up and running, you might like to take time to experiment with these. See Chapter 12 for more on these and other ways of enlivening your pages. And if you want to know more about Java, try *Teach Yourself Java*.

1.4 Tools for the job

You do not need any special software to create simple HTML documents. They can be written on any word-processor or text editor – I normally use either Notepad or WordPad, which will do all that is necessary yet take up little memory. All that is essential is that the software can output plain ASCII text files.

The formatted result can be viewed on your browser, using its **File > Open** command. If your browser is set up so that it goes to your Home page or other Web location on start up, it may be worth changing this while you are developing your HTML files.

Internet Explorer can be set to start on a 'blank page', which stops it from trying to go on-line when the program starts.

To change this setting, open the **Tools** menu and select **Internet Options…**

On the **General** tab in the **Home page** options, click the **Use Blank** button.

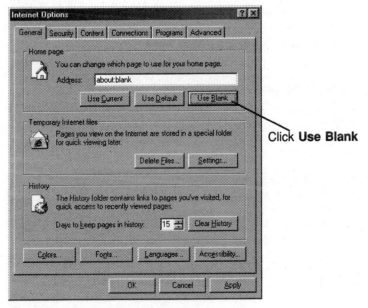

Click **Use Blank**

If you want to include graphics on your page, you should have software that can produce either GIF or JPG files. These are the two most widely used formats – all browsers can display them, and they store images very compactly. Suitable graphics packages are covered in Chapter 3.

When you have created your pages, you will need to upload them to the computer at your Internet service provider – unless you intend to run your own computer as a fully-fledged Web server, which creates all sorts of problems not covered in this book.

You can use Microsoft's Web Publishing Wizard to upload your files, but you get more control with an FTP package – software designed for transferring files in either direction. WS_FTP is the standard Windows software for this. If you do not have a copy, get one from your service provider. We will look at uploading in Chapter 5.

FrontPage

If you intend to create a large and complex Web site, with many pages and graphics files, then you might want to invest in Web builder software such as FrontPage.

This has two main sections. The Editor is a WYSIWYG system that allows you to create and format Web pages, in the same way that you create documents in Word. Its toolbar buttons and menu commands can handle most HTML tags, so that you can format text, or insert links, targets and images very simply. It makes light work of creating tables and forms, both of which – as you will see later – can be quite time-consuming jobs because of the number of tags and options involved.

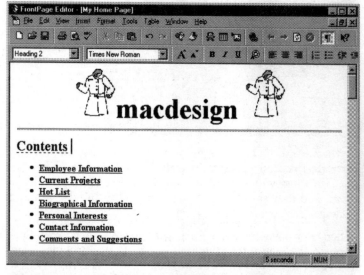

Using the FrontPage Editor to create a Web page. If you are going to create a lot of pages, HTML editing software such as this will save you time – but the DIY approach produces more elegant source code and is much more fun!

The Explorer display gives an overview of the whole structure, showing how pages are linked to each other. You can work through this, focusing on each page in turn, to see which pages are linked to it, and which it leads to – and check that the links are all intact. The overall management of the pages – deleting, moving and relinking them – is also done from here.

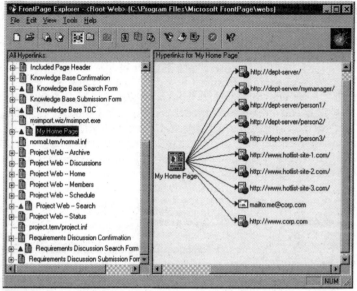

The Explorer display in FrontPage. If your site has more than a couple of dozen pages, keeping the pages – and the links between them – up to date can be a real chore to do by hand. Web management software makes it easier to control your site.

FrontPage Express

FrontPage is not cheap – it's a professional's tool – but if you fancy the idea of an HTML editor, try FrontPage Express. This is a simplified version of FrontPage that used to be supplied with Internet Explorer until recently. It's no longer part of the IE package, though you can still find it on the Web.

FrontPage Express has most of the facilities of the FrontPage Editor. It can handle the full range of text formatting – which can be useful when you want to create intricate text effects. I use it occasionally, mainly for jobs such as setting up a page containing a table – it is much quicker to define the basic table shape and options there than to do it all by hand.

If editors like FrontPage make life so much simpler, why bother with writing HTML yourself? For me, there are three reasons:

● If you really want to understand how Web pages work and what you can do with them, you have to know HTML, and the best way to learn HTML is to write it.

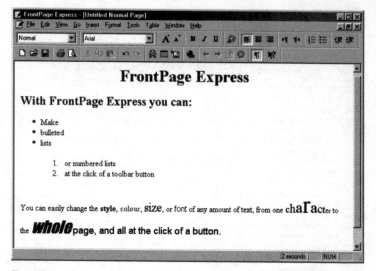

FrontPage Express showing what it can do with text – those changes of style and size took only a few moments to do, but would have meant an awful lot of typing otherwise!

- Unless you pay for proper professional HTML software, such as FrontPage, you do not have the same degree of control over the details of your page, and you cannot use the full range of HTML facilities.

- Even the best editors cannot write HTML code as elegant as yours! They all have extra tags and redundant settings because they cannot see, as you can, what is really necessary. If I've created a page in FrontPage or FrontPage Express, I can usually go into the code afterwards and trim it by 10–20%.

1.5 Learn while you surf

Sometimes you will come across a Web page that makes you say 'This is great! How did they do it?' If you really want to know, you can find out easily enough.

Every Web page has two aspects – the display you see on the screen, and the HTML code that created it. Both are accessible from your browser. In Internet Explorer, use **View > Source** to look at the HTML document. It will be displayed in Internet Explorer's default HTML editor – go to the **Programs** tab of the **Internet Options** panel to choose the editor application.

```
index.html - Notepad
File  Edit  Search  Help
<html>

<head>
<meta http-equiv="Content-Type" ontent="text/html;
charset=iso-8859-1">
<meta name="Classification" content="computing, internet, html,
books, software applications">
<meta name="Description" content="Teach Yourself books on the
Internet, programming and applications">
<meta name="KeyWords" content="Teach Yourself, HTML, computing
books,">
<title>Mac's Home Page</title>
</head>

<body background="stars.gif" text="#FFF000" link="#00FF00"
vlink="#C0C0C0">

<p align="center"><a href="http://www.lateral.ndirect.co.uk"><img
src="machlogo.gif" alt = "Logo" border="0" width="204"
height="56"></a></p>

<h1>Mac's Home Page</h1>

<h1><font size="4">Welcome to my home . Bienvenue . Willkommen .
Mi casa es tu casa . watashi no 'home page' ni youkoso </font></h1>

<hr>
<div align="center">

<table border="5" cellpadding="4" cellspacing="4"
bordercolordark="#808000" bordercolorlight="#FFFF00">
    <tr>
        <td><a href="tybooks.htm"><font size="4">Teach Yourself
        books </font></a></td>
```

My home page when viewed in Notepad. Don't expect it to make much sense yet – it will all become clear as you read on.

You can save the code of any Web page, using **File > Save As....** The document can then be opened in any suitable application.

When you are starting with HTML, you may find that other people's documents do not make much sense. Generally speaking, they were written to be viewed, not read, and the authors have not bothered to add notes, or set out the code in a digestible form. However, it will all become clearer in time.

Note that Internet Explorer offers four **Save as types:**

● *Web page complete,* which stores the page's images and any other embedded files, as well as the HTML document, so that the page can viewed offline.

- *Web archive* stores the same files as the 'complete' option, but in a single file. It is mainly intended for when you want to e-mail a page to a friend.

- *Web page, HTML only* stores the HTML document, but nothing else. Use this if you only want the source code.

- *Text file* stores the displayed text on the page – and not its HTML tags.

Summary

◆ An HTML document is a mixture of plain text and tags, which handle links to other pages, graphics and multimedia clips.

◆ If your service provider does not offer free Web space, find yourself a new provider.

◆ Spend time thinking about what to put on your home page. If you want people to visit, then there should be something there that they want to see.

◆ Apart from your browser and a word-processor, you will need FTP software, and a graphics package would be useful. An HTML editor is not necessary, especially not at first.

◆ You can view the source code for any page on the Web, if you want to see how an effect has been achieved.

02 text and tags

In this unit you will learn

- how tags define HTML documents
- how to format simple text
- how to create a Web page
- how to view your pages in a browser

2.1 HTML tags

Tags are instructions to browsers, telling them how to lay out text, what graphics to display where, what distant pages to link to, and a variety of other things.

Some tags are very simple:

    <H1>

says, 'the next bit of text is to be styled as a level 1 Heading' – i.e. use big type.

Some are much more complex:

    <IMG SRC = "/images/tiddles.gif" ALT = "My cat" WIDTH = 200
    HEIGHT = 100 BORDER = 0 HSPACE = 50 ALIGN = left>

This tells the browser which picture to display, where and how big to display it, and what text to use instead, if the visitor chooses not to download the graphic.

A few basic rules are common to all:

- Each tag must be enclosed in <angle brackets>.
- You can use lower or upper case letters. These are all the same:

    <title>

    <Title>

    <TITLE>

  Upper case makes them stand out better from surrounding text. This can be useful, especially when you are checking through the document to find out why the formatting didn't work properly.

- Most tags come in pairs – one to mark the start of a style, the other to mark its end. The tags in each pair are identical, or the closing tag is a simplified version of the opener, except that the closing tag starts with a / (forward slash), e.g.

    <H1>This is a heading</H1>

- Browsers ignore any spaces or new lines around tags. However, the HTML code will be easier to read if you put spaces around tags, or write them on separate lines. That last example would have been displayed the same on screen if it had been written:

```
<H1>  This is a heading  </H1>
or
<H1>
This is a heading
</H1>
```

2.2 Your first HTML document

Run Notepad, or a word-processor, and start up your browser, but do not go on-line. For the time being, keep the documents on your own computer, and view them with **File > Open**.

Create a new folder for your HTML files. If you keep them all together, you won't waste time hunting for them next time.

<HTML>

Every HTML document starts with the tag:

```
<HTML>
```

and ends with:

```
</HTML>
```

So, at its very simplest, an HTML document might read:

```
<HTML>
This is HTML
</HTML>
```

Type this into your word-processor and save it as a Text file, but with the extension .HTM, e.g. *testpage.htm*.

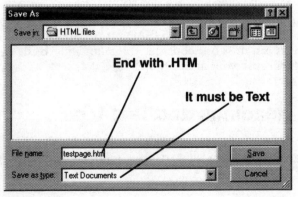

Switch into your browser, use its **File > Open** command and load in your first HTML document. It should look like this.

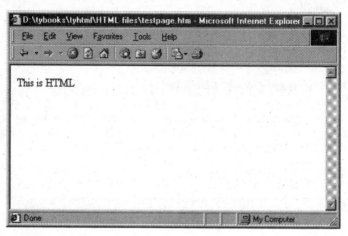

Head and body

An HTML document has two parts: the head and the body. The head part is enclosed by the tags <HEAD> and </HEAD>. Its contents are not displayed on the screen, and are mainly there to identify the Web page. Style information can be written here (see Chapter 11).

The body is enclosed by the tags <BODY> and </BODY>, and its contents form the displayed page. The <BODY> tag can include options to change the colours of the display or add a background image (see pages 34 and 49).

If you don't have anything to put in the head area, you can miss out the <HEAD> and </HEAD> tags. In fact, on a simple page you can miss out both the <HEAD> and <BODY> tags and it will still work perfectly well.

2.3 Headings and text tags

There are a set of tags that can be used to define headings over a range of sizes. They all start <H... followed by a number between 1 and 6.

Type the following into your HTML document, save it and open the file with your browser.

```
<HTML>
<H1> Heading 1 - 24 Point </H1>
<H2> Heading 2 - 18 Point </H2>
<H3> Heading 3 - 14 Point </H3>
<H4> Heading 4 - 12 Point </H4>
<H5> Heading 5 - 10 Point </H5>
<H6> Heading 6 - 7 Point </H6>
Normal body text - 12 Point
</HTML>
```

The resulting display should be something like this.

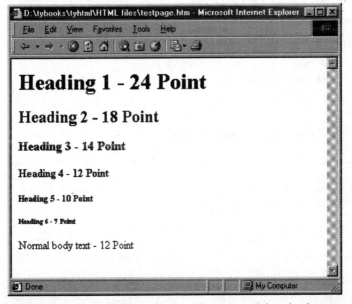

Displays vary because the font is determined by the browser, and this can be changed by the user. How you see your file is not necessarily how other people will see it. Unless they have set their browser up very oddly, an <H1> heading will always be bigger than an <H2>, and so on down the line.

Time-saving tip

If you are testing out tags, and don't want to keep a permanent copy of the document, do a simple **Save** after editing, so that the file keeps the same name. When you switch into your browser, rather than going through the **File > Open** routine, you can simply hit the **Refresh** button.

<TITLE>

Every page should have a title. This is not the text that appears at the top of the page – you do that with a <H1> tag. The title is what appears on the title line of the browser window, and what would be used as a bookmark if anyone bookmarked your page.

It is used in the standard way:

```
<TITLE>
My Home Page
</TITLE>
```

<ADDRESS> </ADDRESS>

These tags have a double effect, setting the text into italic and placing it on a new line. The convention is to use these tags only with your e-mail address. That would normally go at the bottom of your home page.

Edit your HTML test document, or set up a new one, to try out the <TITLE>, <H...> and <ADDRESS> tags. Aim for something along the lines of the one below.

Note the blank lines between sections. They are not necessary – the browser ignores them when it displays the document – but they do make it easier for you to read.

```
<HTML>

<TITLE>
Mac's Home Page
</TITLE>
```

```
<H1>Welcome to my Home </H1>
This page is under construction.
<ADDRESS>
macbride@tcp.co.uk
</ADDRESS>


</HTML>
```

Save the document, open it in a browser, and look at it carefully. If it does not show the title, heading and body text as it should, go back to the word-processor file and check that each tag is properly <bracketed> and has its /closing equivalent.

Title

H1 heading

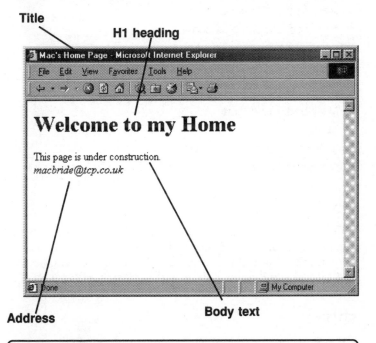

Address

Body text

Word wrap

Text is formatted to suit the size of the browser window, with long lines wrapping round at the right edge. If you change the size of the window, the text is reformatted to fit the new width.

2.4 Paragraphs and breaks

When a browser reads the text in an HTML document, it ignores all excess spaces (only ever displaying one between words), tabs and carriage returns ([Enter] keypresses).

<H...> headings will be placed on separate lines, but if you want to break blocks of body text into paragraphs, or even just start a new line, you have to use one of these three tags.

This is a line BReak and marks the start of a new line.

> Mary had a little lamb
>
> Its fleece was white as snow

will come out as:

> Mary had a little lambIts fleece was white as snow

To get separate lines you must use

> Mary had a little lamb
>
>
>
> Its fleece was white as snow

Note that <BR> stands alone – there is no closing tag.

<P>

This marks the start of a new paragraph, and places a blank line before it. You can equally well place it at the end of a piece of text, at the start of the next, or in between. <P> can be used as a second stand-alone tag, or with a closing </P>.

<HR>

HR stands for Horizontal Rule. This stand-alone tag separates paragraphs by drawing a line between them. The basic line will be thin, with a shaded effect, and extend almost the full width of the window. This can be changed (see page 96).

You can see these three tags at work in the next example.

Substitute your own text, but follow the pattern of tags.

```
<HTML>
<HEAD>
<TITLE>
Ingrid's Home Page
</TITLE>
</HEAD>
<BODY>
<H1> A big hello from Ingrid Bottomlow </H1>
<HR>
<H2> Me and my family </H2>
I am the only daughter of Gnoah and Gnora Bottomlow.
<BR>
I have four brothers - Bumpy, Dumpy, Gnoggin and Jonah.
<H2> Where I live </H2>
I live with my family at Gnettlefield Farm, outside Little
Moaning.
<P>
The River Dribble flows past, and sometimes through, our farm.
</BODY>
</HTML>
```

H1 heading

Drawn line

H2 heading

Line break

Paragraph

Design with text

With six levels of headings, paragraph and line breaks, you
have enough to be able to produce clear, well-formatted
text. Experiment and see if this is enough to be able to get
your message across adequately. If it is, you can skip to
Chapter 5 and put your home page on the Web. If you want
more variety in your text, or you want to include graphics or
links to other pages, then curb your desire to be published,
and read on.

Ingrid's page looks like this. She is exempt from the don't-just-write-about-yourself rule as she is a celebrity – at least to those who remember Level 9 games.

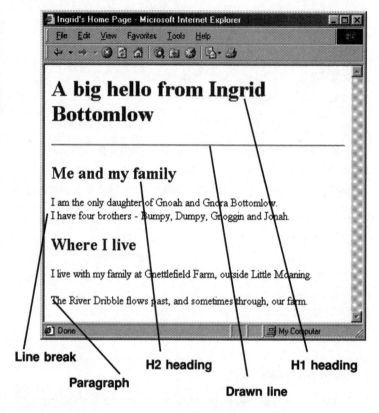

Line break

Paragraph

H2 heading

Drawn line

H1 heading

2.5 Further text formatting

<FONT SIZE = value>

The <H...> tags are a simple but effective way of creating head-ings, but if you want more control over the size of heading text, or want to vary the size of text *within* a paragraph, you must use the <FONT SIZE = ... > tag.

The SIZE value can be from 7 down to 2, with 7 the largest size, at 36 points. Note that the values run in the opposite direction to the headings, where <H1> is the largest.

FONT SIZE	Heading	Point size
7	–	36 pt
6	<H1>	24 pt
5	<H2>	18 pt
4	<H4>	12 pt bold
3	Body text	12 pt plain
2	–	9 pt

For headings, it is simpler to use the <H...> tags – unless you want a huge 36 point heading. Keep the <FONT SIZE = ... > tag for special effects.

To turn off a font size, either set a new <FONT SIZE = ...> or use </FONT> to revert to the previous size.

Try this:

```
<HTML>

<FONT SIZE = 4> A big <FONT SIZE = 7> Hello </FONT>
from me
</HTML>          Or you could write <FONT SIZE = 4>
```

I haven't given the code for this 'roller coaster ride' – you can work it out. All it needs is a <FONT SIZE = > before every letter!

Aligning text

Body text and headings are normally aligned to the left edge, but both can be set in the centre or to the right, if required.

To set the alignment, you write inside the <H ...> or <P> tag the keyword ALIGN = followed by *Center*, *Right* or *Left*. (Left is never needed – a simple <P> will left align text – but it can sometimes help to make the coding easier to read.) When text is used as an option value, as here, it can be enclosed in double quotes. This is only essential when the text consists of two or more words.

For example:

    <H2 ALIGN = "Right">

starts a right aligned heading. <H2> closes it.

    <P ALIGN = "Center">

makes the following paragraph align to the centre of the window.

Note that the US spelling CEN<u>TER</u> must be used in the tags.

Quotes in options

Where you are setting an option, such as ALIGN = "Left", the quotes are not essential, but can be added for improved readability. You can also use any mix of lower case and capitals. ALIGN = LEFT, align = left, Align = "Left" all work.

This example demonstrates the ALIGN clause in action.

    <HTML>
    <BODY>
    <H1 ALIGN = "Center"> Text Alignment</H1>
    <P ALIGN = "Center">
    Set in the centre of the window

    As many lines as you like from one ALIGN
    <P>
    Back to normal

```
<P ALIGN = "Right">
Align to the right
<P ALIGN = "Left">
Align to the left. This is the same as not setting an ALIGN
option. Note that long lines wrap round to fit the window size.
</BODY>
</HTML>
```

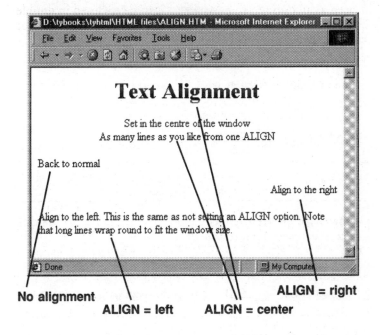

No alignment

ALIGN = left   **ALIGN = center**

ALIGN = right

<!Comments>

Every HTML document has two aspects. There is the displayed page that the world will see, and the underlying source code, which is mainly of interest to you. If you want to add comments to the document, for your use and not for general consumption, write them inside <!...> tags, like this:

<! Written by me, with help from Harry>

<! Last modified 27/6/2002>

<!...> is used in the next example.

Adding emphasis

If you want to emphasize a word or phrase in your text, you can use these pairs of tags.

<B> </B>

Sets text to **bold**.

<I> </I>

Makes text *italic*.

<TT> </TT>

This creates a 'typewriter' effect, by setting text in `Courier`.

These tags can be seen at work in the next example. This also demonstrates the use of an <!...> tag to write a hidden credit into the head of the document.

<STRONG> </STRONG>

<B>, <I> and <TT> are *physical* tags – they only work if the visitor's browser can display bold, italic or Courier fonts. <STRONG> is an example of a *logical* tag – one whose effect can be redefined at the receiving end. In practice, it will usually have the same emboldening effect as <B>. The subtle differences between logical and physical tags can be left to the experts.

<EM> </EM>

The EMPHASIS tag is the logical equivalent to <I>, and has the advantage of being more easily spotted when you are checking through your code for mistakes.

The other logical tags are **<CITE>**, **<CODE>** and **<KBD>**. They are all used in the same way as **<STRONG>**.

Superscript and subscript

You can also use the tags for superscript and for subscript.

Try this HTML code to see the effect of the styling tags.

```
<HTML>
<HEAD>
<TITLE> Emphasis in Text </Title>
```

<! Written 24/7/2002> ——————— **Comment**

</HEAD>

<BODY>

<H2> Emphasizing Text </H2>

If you set words in <B> bold </B> or <STRONG> Strong </STRONG> they stand out well.

<P>

<I> Italics </I> or <EM> Emphasis </EM> give more subtle emphasis.

<P>

To really make words <B> <I> leap out </I> </B> use both

<P>

For something different, try <TT> typewriter </TT>

<P>

Feedback to:

<ADDRESS>macbride@tcp.co.uk</ADDRESS>

</BODY>

</HTML>

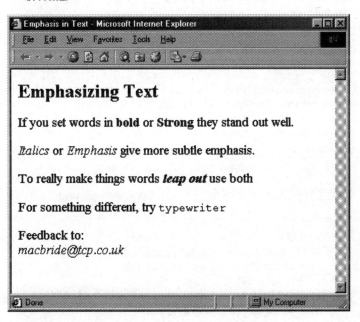

Emphasis in Text - Microsoft Internet Explorer

File Edit View Favorites Tools Help

Emphasizing Text

If you set words in **bold** or **Strong** they stand out well.

Italics or *Emphasis* give more subtle emphasis.

To really make things words ***leap out*** use both

For something different, try `typewriter`

Feedback to:
macbride@tcp.co.uk

Done   My Computer

2.6 Preformatted text

We noted earlier that when browsers display HTML documents, they ignore all spaces and new lines (and tabs). Most of the time this is a good thing, as it means that you can spread out your source code so that you can read it easily, while the tags create a displayed page which is easy for your visitors to read.

We have already covered the paragraph formatting tags, <P> and <BR>. There are more tags that can be used to create lists and tables, and we will come on to these later. First, there's another way to format text that is worth a quick look.

<PRE> </PRE>

These tags define preformatted text, and tell the browser to include the spaces, tabs and new lines, just as they are written. Within the <PRE> block, text is displayed in Courier. Unlike most fonts, Courier does *not* have proportional spacing. Instead every letter and space occupies the same width on screen. This means that you can use spaces to push text over to the right – and get it exactly where you want it. Tags are still obeyed, within the <PRE> block, so you can include headings, font sizes and alignments as usual.

Use <PRE> for price lists, poems, or other text where the pattern of tabs and spaces is important.

In this example, notice the pattern of indents and the right-aligned price list. Note also that the <H...> tags and ALIGN setting produce their usual effects.

```
<HTML>
<HEAD>
<TITLE>Preformatted text</TITLE>
</HEAD>
                              Centred heading
<BODY>
<PRE>
<H3 ALIGN = "Center"> Rent-a-Rhyme </H3>
      There was a young netter called Seb
      Who put his Home page on the Web
            He said "What a drag
            I've missed out a tag      2 levels of indents
      The nerds will all think I'm a pleb"
```

```
<H4>Unbeatable prices!</H4>
      Limericks          4.99
      Clerihews          10.49
      Doggerel                25p per line
      Sonnets            39.99
      Free Verse         £POA
</PRE>
</BODY>
</HTML>
```

prices lined up here

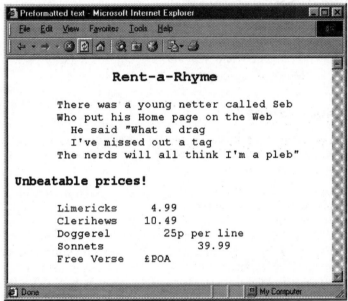

The <TABLE> facility (Chapter 8) lets you produce clear and attractive tables, but <PRE>formatting is a quick way to display columns of data.

Spaces in code

Remember that the browser ignores extra spaces, except in <PRE> blocks. This means that you can happily put spaces around tags to make them more visible in your code, without creating nasty gaps on screen.

2.7 Colour

If you have tried out the examples so far, you may have noticed that the text appears in black on a white background. This is nice and clear, but you don't have to stick with these colours.

<BODY BGCOLOR = *value* TEXT = *value* >

You can set the colour of the background and of the text, by including either or both phrases in the <BODY ...> tag. These settings apply to the whole document.

<FONT COLOR = *value*>

This changes the colour of text, just as <FONT SIZE = ...> sets its size. Likewise, when you have done with a colour, you can switch to a new one with another <FONT COLOR = ... > tag, or restore the previous colour with </FONT>.

Colour values

Colours can be specified in two ways. There are standard names which you can use to identify 16 basic colours – this is the simplest approach, and should be fine for most purposes.

If you are feeling more adventurous, you can define any colour by giving its 6-digit hexadecimal number. This actually splits into three numbers, each of two digits, which set the brightness of the Red, Green and Blue components – in that order. The value can be anything between '00' and 'FF', but the subtle differences between your carefully crafted colours will be lost on any visitor who doesn't have a high colour screen. In practical terms, it is enough to think of the light values as being '00' for *off*, '80' for *dipped* and 'FF' for *full beam*.

RGB colour

On a colour monitor, colours are produced by combining Red, Green and Blue light. Crudely, they combine like this:

	'Full Beam'	'Dipped'
Red + Green	Yellow	Brown
Red + Blue	Lilac	Magenta (Purple)
Green + Blue	Cyan	Turquoise
Red + Green + Blue	White	Grey

By varying the intensity of the three colours, you can produce the whole range of colours, and the intensity can be varied on a scale of 0 (off) to 255 (full beam). Except, you have to use hexadecimal. Time for digression number 2.

Hexadecimal

People naturally work in denary (base 10) because they have 10 fingers. Computers naturally work with binary (base 2) numbers, because they have two electronic 'fingers' – on and off. Binary numbers are dreadful for people to handle. (Read these aloud: 01001011 and 01011010. See what I mean?)

Hexadecimal (base 16) is a compromise choice. The numbers can be converted easily into binary ($16 = 2 \times 2 \times 2 \times 2$) and can be read easily be people. The key point to note about hexadecimal is that it uses 16 'fingers', so the digits '0' to '9' are not enough. The letters 'A' to 'F' are pressed into service.

Base 10	Hex		Base 10	Hex	
0	0		17	11	
1	1		18	12	
2	2		19	13	
3	3		20	14	
4	4		21	15	
5	5		22	16	
6	6		23	17	
7	7		24	18	
8	8		25	19	
9	9		26	1A	
10	A		27	1B	
11	B		28	1C	
12	C		29	1D	
13	D		30	1E	
14	E		31	1F	
15	F		32	20	
16	10	(a 'handful')	33	21	etc.

Hexadecimal numbers are usually written as a pair of digits. To work out their base 10 value, multiply the first by 16 and add the second. For example:

2B	$= 2 \times 16 + 11(B)$	$= 43$
80	$= 8 \times 16 + 0$	$= 128$
FF	$= 15(F) \times 16 + 15$	$= 255$

FF is the biggest number you can write with 2 digits. It is also the biggest value that can be held in 1 byte.

If a standard colour will do the job, it can be specified by name. Here are the standard colour names and their RGB values:

R	G	B	Colour name
00	00	00	Black
FF	00	00	Red
00	FF	00	Lime
00	00	FF	Blue
FF	FF	00	Yellow
FF	00	FF	Fuchsia
00	FF	FF	Aqua
FF	FF	FF	White
80	00	00	Maroon
00	80	00	Green
00	00	80	Navy
80	00	80	Purple
80	80	00	Olive
00	80	80	Teal
80	80	80	Gray *
C0	C0	C0	Silver

* Note the US spelling

To set default colours for the whole document, use the keywords 'BGCOLOR = ' and 'TEXT = ' with the appropriate values, inside the <BODY ....> tag.

To set the colour for a section of text, use the keywords 'COLOR = ' inside a <FONT ...> tag.

Note the US spelling – COLOR and BGCOLOR.

By convention, the values are written in quotes with a preceding hash (#). These help to make the numbers stand out, but neither # nor quotes are necessary. Capital or lower case letters can be used for the hexadecimal digits A–F. These all produce the same pale yellow:

```
"#FFFF80"      "#ffff80"

FFFF80         ffff80
```

Examples:
```
<BODY BGCOLOR = "#80000">
```
or
```
<BODY BGCOLOR = "Maroon">
```
sets the background to dark red.
```
<BODY TEXT = 0000FF>
```
or
```
<BODY TEXT = blue>
```
sets the text colour to bright blue.
```
<BODY BGCOLOR = 000000 TEXT = FFFF00>
```
or
```
<BODY BGCOLOR = black TEXT = Yellow>
```
sets the background to black and the text to yellow.
```
<FONT COLOR = "#808080"> Donkey </FONT>
```
sets "Donkey" in grey, then reverts to the previous colour.

Use code like this to test out the range of colours:

```
<HTML>
<HEAD>
<TITLE>Colour test</TITLE>          set colours at the start
</HEAD>
<BODY BGCOLOR = "#FFFFFF" TEXT = "#000000">
<H1>Colour test</H1>               COLOR – US spelling!
<FONT SIZE = 5>
Let's get bright and cheerful
<BR><FONT COLOR = "#FF0000"> Red
<BR><FONT COLOR = "#00FF00"> Green    colour within
<BR><FONT COLOR = "#0000FFv> Blue     the body text
<BR></FONT>Back to green, </FONT> then to red,
</FONT> then to black
</BODY>                    closing tag
</HTML>
```

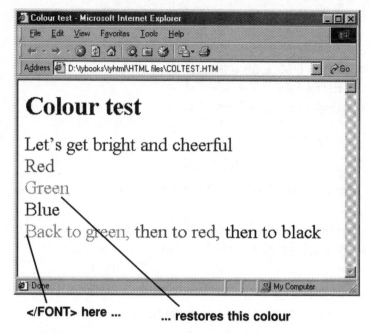

</FONT> here ...   **... restores this colour**

I couldn't persuade the publishers to print this page in colour, but the shades of grey indicate the colour changes. Notice how the </FONT> tags switch back to the previous colour, not to the one set by the <BODY TEXT = ...> option.

Link colours

We will cover links in Chapter 4, but there is one aspect of them which is worth picking up now. Links are normally displayed in blue, if they have not yet been used, or purple if they have. If you change the colour of your background, or of your text, links may not stand out as well as you would like.

    <BODY ... LINK = *value* ALINK = *value* VLINK = *value*>

Any or all of these options can be used to set the colour of the text that leads to:

    an unvisited link (LINK),
    the active link (ALINK),
    a visited link (VLINK).

The colour values are the same as for other settings.

Summary

◆ There are simple, standard rules that apply to HTML tags.

◆ Most tags are used in pairs, with a </Closing tag> being used to mark the end of a formatted block.

◆ HTML documents can be written in Notepad or any word processor, but must be saved as plain text, with the .HTM extension to the filename.

◆ The <H...> tags provide a simple way to create headings. They set the size of text, embolden it and place it on a separate line.

◆ Use the <ADDRESS> pair of tags to add your e-mail address to the end of your document.

◆ Browsers normally ignore carriage returns, tabs and all excess spaces.

◆ Body text can be divided into paragraphs by the <P> tag, or placed on separate lines by inserting a <BR> break.

◆ You can control the size of words or single characters within the text using the SIZE = option in a <FONT> tag.

◆ You can add comments to code by putting them in a <! ...> tag. Anything written in these will not be displayed.

◆ Body text and headings can be aligned to left, right or centre using the ALIGN = options.

◆ For emphasis, you can set your text in bold, italics or use a typewriter effect.

◆ Where you want to retain the spaces, tabs and carriage returns in your layout, use the <PRE> pair of tags to define it as preformatted text.

◆ The colour of the background and text for the whole document can be set by options in the <BODY> tag.

◆ The colour of words and characters within the text can be set by the COLOR = option in a <FONT> tag.

◆ The colours used to identify link text can be set by the LINK, ALINK, VLINK options in the <BODY> tag.

03 graphics

In this unit you will learn

- how to include an image
  in a page
- how to control the placing
  and scale of images
- how to use an image as a
  background
- about file formats

3.1 Linking an image

<IMG SRC = "filename">

<IMG SRC ...> (IMaGe SouRCe) is the basic tag for linking an image into your page. Used without qualification, it places the image against the left edge, directly after any text, and with later text starting to its right.

For example:

```
<HTML>
<H2>Graphics</H2>
<IMG SRC = "ggnome.gif">
The Green Gnome
<P>My brother Gnoggin spends far too much time there!
</HTML>
```

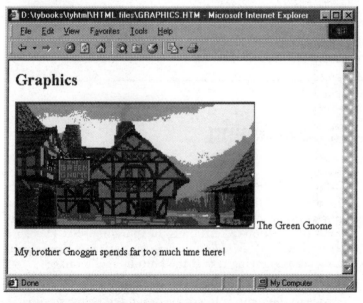

Note that following text will normally start at the lower right of the image. A <P> tag would push it onto the next line, or you could use an ALIGN qualifier – see below.

If the file is in the same folder as the HTML document, you only have to give its name – that was the case in the example above. If the image is stored elsewhere, you will have to include the path to the folder.

In HTML, the path does not follow Windows rules. HTML was originally designed for Unix machines and it expects paths written the Unix way. Use forward slashes not backslashes, between folder names, and start with a forward slash. You also need to use a vertical bar line (|) and a slash, in place of the colon after the drive letter.

If you had a graphic MYPIC.GIF in a folder whose Windows path was C:\WINDOWS\TEMP, its HTML path would read:

/C|/WINDOWS/TEMP/MYPIC.GIF

That /forward slash at the start is essential.

Tip

Make life easy for yourself. While you are testing ideas, keep your graphics in the same folder as your HTML documents. When you put your page up on the Web, put all the files into one folder (see Chapter 5).

3.2 Positioning

ALIGN =

You have seen ALIGN used with the <P> and <H...> tags to align text to the left, right and centre. Used with images, it sets the vertical position in relation to surrounding text. There are three options: *Top*, *Middle* and *Bottom*. *Bottom* is the default, placing accompanying text at the bottom of the image.

If there is following text, and it is too long to fit in the remaining space to the right, it is wrapped round to below the image.

```
<HTML>
<BODY>
<H2>Graphics - Alignment</H2>
```

```
<FONT SIZE = 4>
Text before                      Quotes are optional but
                                 make names stand out
<IMG SRC = "arrows.gif" ALIGN = Middle>
Text after. Long sentences wrap round to below the image
</FONT>
</BODY>
</HTML>
```

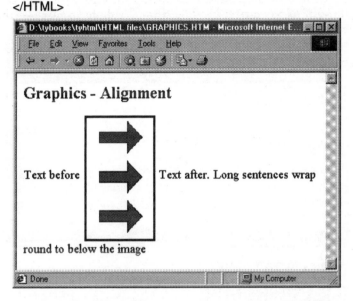

If you want to title your image, a *<H...>* tag will push the heading onto a new line. Use *FONT SIZE* to place enlarged text beside the image. Where text is so long that it will wrap round below the image, use *ALIGN = Bottom*. *ALIGN = Middle* looks a mess, as you can see, *ALIGN = Top* is even worse! Alternatively, use a table to set a block of text alongside an image – see Chapter 8.

<CENTER>

When looking at text alignment in the last chapter, we met the ALIGN = "Center" option for paragraphs and headings. <CENTER> can also be used as a tag in its own right to align text *and graphics* in the centre of the display window. When used in this way, a closing </CENTER> tag is needed at the end of the centred material.

For example:

```
<HTML>
<BODY>
<H3>Positioning Graphics</H3>
<CENTER><IMG SRC = "smiley.gif"></CENTER>
</BODY>
</HTML>
```

CENTER – US spelling

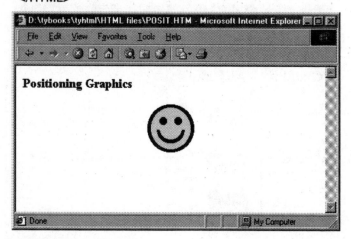

If this had been written:

```
<HTML>
<BODY>
<CENTER>
<H3>Positioning Graphics</H3>
<IMG SRC = "smiley.gif"></CENTER>
</BODY>
</HTML>
```

both the heading and image would have been centred.

Spacing

There are two options that can control the spacing around graphics. The default settings are to leave a space of 10 pixels above and below an image, and about 6 pixels to either side.

HSPACE = sets the spacing (in pixels) to the left and right;
VSPACE = sets the spacing above and below the image.

You cannot control left and right, or above and below spacing
independently.

Unless you are aiming for a particularly 'spaced-out' look, the
HSPACE and VSPACE values should not be too large. In the
example below they have been exaggerated so that their effects
are clearly visible. Compare these with the first two graphics,
which are placed at the default spacing.

```
<HTML>
<HEAD>
<TITLE>Graphics Spacing</TITLE>
</HEAD>
<BODY BGCOLOR = 80FF80 TEXT = 00008F>
<IMG SRC = "arrow1.gif" ALIGN = Middle> Buy now! <P>
<IMG SRC = "arrow1.gif" ALIGN = Middle> Huge savings!<P>
```

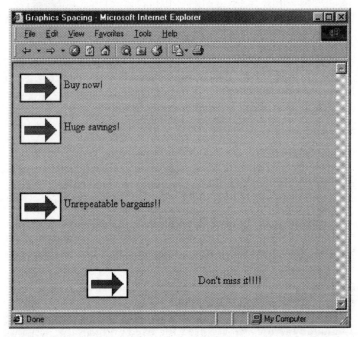

Space around graphics makes them stand out, but don't overdo it!

<IMG SRC = "arrow1.gif" ALIGN = Middle VSPACE = 25>
Unrepeatable bargains!! <P>

<IMG SRC = "arrow1.gif" ALIGN = Middle HSPACE = 50>
Don't miss it!!!!

</BODY>

</HTML>

Borders

You can put a border around an image by including the
option BORDER = ... setting the thickness in pixels. e.g.

<IMG SRC = "mypic.gif" ALIGN = Middle BORDER = 5>

3.3 Adjusting the size

Normally you would want your graphics to be displayed at
their natural size, but there are some times when it is useful to
be able to adjust the size of the displayed image. There is little
point in showing an image at a reduced size – you may as well
make it smaller to start with, and save the reduced image to
file. If you make the display larger than the original, it keeps
down the size of the graphics file and the download time, but
it will produce a lower resolution, chunkier image. This won't
matter if the original picture was simple and chunky anyway,
but is not advisable for photographs or scanned art.

HTML gives us two alternative ways of setting the size:

- fixed, where the displayed size is given in pixels – it helps
  if you know the size of the original;
- variable, where the size is specified as a percentage of the
  screen size.

The advantage of the variable approach is that you can be sure
that your image will fit on screen, whatever the size of your
visitors' windows. We'll come back to that in our second example.

HEIGHT = *value* WIDTH = *value*

The same tag options are used for fixed and variable resizing.
The only difference is in how you give the values.

For **fixed** sizing, simply give the pixels as plain numbers:

HEIGHT = 100 WIDTH = 75

sets the displayed size of the image at 100 x 75 pixels. If you want to avoid distorting the shape, you must know the original pixel size, so that you can calculate the new values.

For **variable** sizing, give the value as a percentage of the screen height or width, and follow the number with a % sign.

HEIGHT = 50%

sets the image to be scaled down so that it fills half the height of the browser window.

WIDTH = 25%

scales the image down to fit into a quarter of the width of the window.

If you only set one value, the same scaling is applied in both directions. Set HEIGHT *and* WIDTH only if it is essential that the image occupies a certain amount of space in both directions – you can guarantee that few of your visitors will be using the same shape of browser window as you, so that most will get a distorted image.

```
<HTML>
<HEAD>
<TITLE>Graphics Sizing</TITLE>
</HEAD>

<BODY BGCOLOR = FFFFFF>
<IMG SRC = "compass.gif"> Original size 60 x 60
<IMG SRC = "compass.gif" HEIGHT = 90 WIDTH = 90>
Increased to 90 x 90 <BR>
<IMG SRC = "compass.gif" HEIGHT = 50%> Sized to fill half
of the screen height <BR>
<IMG SRC = "compass.gif" WIDTH = 10%> Sized to fill a
tenth of the width
</BODY>
</HTML>
```

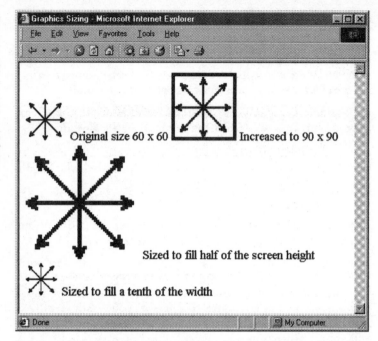

Enlarged (or reduced) images rarely look as good as the originals.

If you want to start your page with a bang, you can use a graphic instead of a <H ...> heading. Even if you only use text, at least you can have coloured text and set in any font that your computer can produce. With a normal <H ...> heading, it will be wrapped round if your visitor is working in a narrow window. With a graphic as a heading, there is a danger that half of it will disappear off the edge of a visitor's window. And this is where percentage resizing really comes into its own. In the example below, the title will always occupy 80% of the width of the window – whatever that width is.

```
<HTML>
<BODY BGCOLOR = FFFFFF>
<CENTER>
<IMG SRC = "grafhead.gif" WIDTH = 80%>
<H2>Web Weavers Hand-knitted T-shirts</H2>
</CENTER>
<P>
```

For that perfect fit in T-shirts, order yours now from Web
Weavers.

```
<P>
<BODY>
</HTML>
```

With percentage
scaling, you always
get a perfect fit for
your graphics.

3.4 Background images

Another striking use for an image is as a background to your
page. The trick here is *not* to use a large, full-page picture –
which will take an age to download – but to use a small image.
HTML automatically repeats any image used as a background,
so you can get a full screen from the tiniest images.

With any kind of background pattern, it is important that the
pattern does not become too dominant – it is supposed to be a

background after all. The answer is either to use a very sparse pattern, or pale colours. You can see examples of both here.

This first page has a 'deep space' background, formed by repeating this scatter of stars. The original image is about 200 pixels square, and as a GIF file, takes less than 500 bytes. Used with bright yellow or cyan text, it is striking, but still produces a readable page.

```
<HTML>
<HEAD>
<TITLE>
BACKGROUND GRAPHICS
</TITLE>
</HEAD>
<BODY>
<BODY BACKGROUND = "stars.gif" TEXT = FFFF00>
<FONT SIZE = 7>
One for the Star Trek fans
<FONT SIZE = 5>
<P>
The simpler the background, the better
</BODY>
</HTML>
```

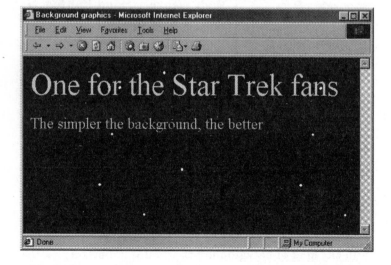

The second example uses a proper pattern. This one is based on the TRIANGLES.BMP, one of the 'wallpapers' supplied with Windows. The original image is minute 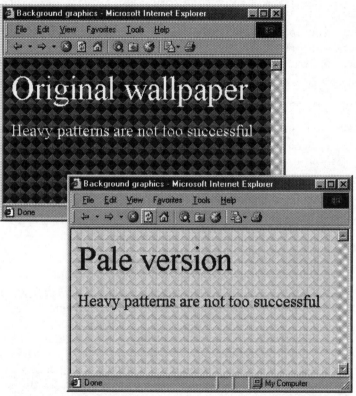 – but it tiles to good effect. It also has strong contrasts, which is not so good. Whether you use dark or light text, parts of it will be unreadable against some areas of the pattern.

Simplifying the colour range and using lighter colours produce a better result.

Look out for background images as you surf the Web. You can see the star pattern and others at the *Teach Yourself HTML* test site:

homepages.tcp.co.uk/~macbride/tybooks.htm

3.5 File formats

Web standards

You may have noticed that in the examples so far, I have used GIF files. GIF (Graphic Information Format) was established by CompuServe as the standard for graphics used in their communication services. It was chosen because its built-in compression produces very compact files. For this same reason it has been adopted as a standard for Web browsers.

GIF files can only handle 256 colours. This is fine for drawings, cartoons and background images, but is not enough to display photographs properly. For these, you need to use the JPEG (Joint Photographic Experts Group) format – on PCs the files have a JGP extension. This also produces compact files, but can cope with 16 million colour images.

Both GIF and JPG formats can be displayed directly in Web browsers. Your visitors will only be able to see graphics in other formats if they have suitable external viewers.

Other formats

Someone once commented that the computing industry must love standards as they have so many of them! This is certainly true with graphic 'standard' formats. There are dozens of them. On a Windows system, without any other software, you can produce graphics in four different BMP formats, and as GIF files. If you have installed the PhotoEditor that is supplied with Windows, or have attached a digital camera or scanner to your computer and installed its software, then you will be able to produce JPEGs.

Check the graphics applications on your computer to see what formats they can save images in. If you do not have programs that can output GIF and JPEG files, for any reason, you need to get hold of suitable software.

Graphics software

There are a number of freeware, shareware and commercial programs for converting graphics between formats. They are regularly given away on magazine-cover CDs, and there's a good selection of low-cost and free software available on-line. Have a browse at CNET's shareware site sometime:

http://cnet.shareware.com

Search for 'graphics software' and follow the leads.

//www.completelyfreesoftware.com/

Summary

◆ Images can be placed in a page with the <IMG SRC = ...> tag.

◆ The ALIGN = option can be used to align following text with the top, middle or bottom of an image.

◆ Images can be centred on a page with <CENTER>.

◆ The space around an image can be adjusted with the HSPACE = and VSPACE = options.

◆ The size of an image can be fixed, or made relative to the browser window size, using the WIDTH = and HEIGHT = options.

◆ The <BODY BACKGROUND = ...> option allows you to fill the background of the page with a single image, or a repeated pattern of a small image.

◆ All browsers can display graphics in GIF or JPG formats. Other formats create problems.

◆ Modern Windows systems should already have suitable software for producing files in GIF or JPEG format. There are also many free or cheap packages available through the Web.

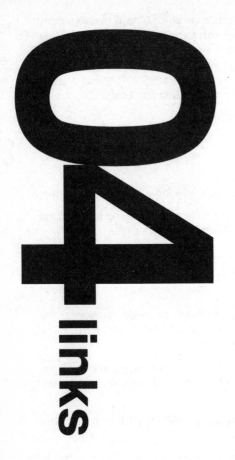

04 links

In this unit you will learn

- how to create links to other pages
- how to create links within a page
- how to use images to hold links
- how to link to e-mail and to files off the Web

4.1 HREF

The key word for links is HREF (Hypertext REFerence). This identifies the target page, or point within a page. But it can't be used by itself. It must be anchored to a piece of text or a graphic, so that there is something to click on to pick up the link. The *anchor* tags are <A ...> and </A> which mark the start and end of the link text.

The two are used together to create the link and its jumping off point. For example:

    <A HREF = "http://www.yahoo.com"> Go to Yahoo </A>

Let's break that down:

<A HREF =	marks the start of the tag.
http://	identifies it as a World Wide Web link. You could miss this out and the link would still work – browsers assume that a link is to a Web page unless they are told differently. But if you do want another type of link, you must include its identifier (see page 66).
www.yahoo.com	the URL of the target – this is the home page of the Yahoo! directory.
Go to Yahoo	is the link text that will be underlined when viewed in a browser, and can be clicked to make the connection.
</A>	marks the end of the link text.

You can use different types of links, and replace the text by an image, but all hypertext links follow this pattern.

URLs

Every page, file, directory, site and person on the Internet has its URL – Uniform Resource Locator. The basic pattern is the same:

    type://HostComputerAddress/Directory/Filename

Type	Identifies
http://	Web page
file://	file in a local directory
ftp://	file that can be downloaded via FTP
news://	link to a newsgroup
mailto://	e-mail address of a person

4.2 Links to other pages

These are the simplest to handle, especially where the link is to the home page of a well-established site. Just use the http:// identifier (you can even miss it out) and give the address as in the example opposite.

Here are some more examples – and they are to places that you should have in your own Bookmark file:

```
<A HREF = "http://www.google.com"> Google </A>
<A HREF = "http://www.yahoo.com"> Yahoo! </A>
<A HREF = "http://www.shareware.com"> cnet Shareware </A>
```

Google is my favourite search engine, and where I go when I'm looking for any kind of information. Yahoo! is the leading Web directory. As well as the main one, there are Yahoos in most countries, e.g. www.yahoo.co.uk (UK), hk.yahoo.com (Hong Kong), no.yahoo.com (Norway) – you might prefer to link to your local site. cnet Shareware is an excellent source of freeware and shareware.

If you are linking to a page or file in a sub-directory, or to the home page of another user, then there are two points that need special attention.

● You must get the page address absolutely right – using upper and lower case and punctuation exactly according to the URL.

● You must check the link regularly to make sure that it is still there. People have a nasty habit of reorganising their directories, or moving from one service to another, just after you have included the link in your page!

Exact addresses

The first step in setting up any link is to get the exact address. The best way to do that is to go there yourself – which guarantees that you have the address right – then copy the address from the Location slot at the top of the browser.

If you highlight it and use **Edit|Copy**, rather than copying it by hand, you can be sure of not making a mistake. The address can then be pasted into your HTML document.

Edit/Copy the address and *Paste* it into your document

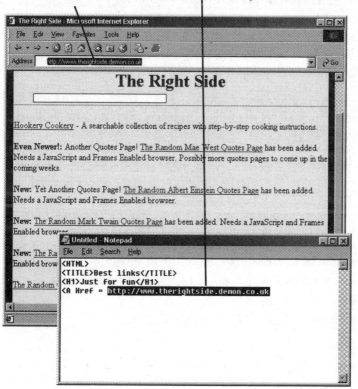

The Copy and Paste approach avoids all errors, but may not always be convenient – you may not want to start editing an HTML document half way through a surfing session. Just make sure you write down addresses exactly as you see them.

In particular, watch out for:

- the use of underlines and capital letters
  http://www.yahoo.com/Computers_and_Internet
  this is the Computers and Internet menu at Yahoo.
- tildes (~), used to indicate an individual user's page
  http://homepages.tcp.co.uk/~macbride/tybooks.html
  my 'Teach Yourself books' page at Total Connectivity Providers.

Your other pages

OK! I know you haven't got your first home page up yet, un-less you have skipped ahead, but let's do this while we are on links.

If you do not have a lot to say, a single page will do the job, but it is a different matter if you want to publish a lot of information, or cover several distinct areas – you, your job, your hobby and your holiday snaps; your firm's four product lines; the two clubs that you run; separate home pages for you, your partner, your kids, your granny and your cat ... or whatever. These could all result in long, slow-to-download pages. A better solution is to have several pages, all accessible from the top one. Your visitors can then go quickly to the page that interests them.

The pages should all be stored in the same directory – now, on your system while you are testing them, and later when you upload them to your service provider. The link is then a very simple one, consisting only of the filename:

```
<A HREF = "tiddles.htm"> My Cat's Home Page </A>
```

The linked pages, in a multi-page set should all have a link back to the top-level home page.

Here's a skeleton set:

The top level. Filename = *index.html*

```
<HTML>
<HEAD>
<TITLE> My Home Page </TITLE>
</HEAD>
<BODY>
...
<A HREF = "myjob.htm"> My Job </A>
<A HREF = "myhobby.htm"> My Hobby </A>
<A HREF = "links.htm"> Favourite Places </A>
<A HREF = "author.htm"> All about me </A>
...
</BODY>
</HTML>
```

Linked page. Filename = *myjob.htm*

```
<HTML>
<HEAD>
<TITLE> My Job </TITLE>
</HEAD>
<BODY>
I work for .......
<A HREF = "index.html"> Return to the top </A>
</BODY>
</HTML>
```

Come up and see me sometime

For a more fully worked example of a multi-page set, drop in on my home page:

homepages.tcp.co.uk/~macbride

4.3 Links within a page

If you want to jump from one part of a page to another – perhaps from a menu at the top, down to a section, or back up to the top – you have to define the points to jump to. These are marked by a variation on the anchor tag:

```
<A NAME = jumppoint> jump point text </A>
```

The jump point can be a single word or phrase, and you can write it in quotes if you want to make it stand out more clearly in the source code. It will not be identified in the display – there is no reason to do so, as this is a place that you arrive at, not somewhere to go from. The <A NAME = ...> tag can therefore be wrapped around an existing heading, or embedded in body text at the right place.

These are both acceptable uses:

```
<A NAME = my job> I work </A> for .....
<A NAME = "backup"> Welcome </A>
```

At the jumping-off point, use an HREF tag, as with other links:

```
<A HREF = #jumppoint> text </A>
```

Notice the hash (#) before the *jumppoint* name. It is crucial. If you miss it out, the browser will think that you are trying to make a simple link to another page in your directory.

As with other links, it is vital to use exactly the same punctuation and upper/lower case characters in the HREF as in the NAME.

```
<A HREF = #Me> All About Me </A>
```

will not find:

```
<A NAME = "me"> I am </A> nearly 9 and have surfed for...
```

because "me" and "Me" are two different things.

In the example below, the home page will have four sections, when it is finished. At this stage, the first two are in place and can be jumped to from the Contents list at the top.

Notice that both have jumps at the end to take the visitor back up to the top of the page.

```
<HTML>
<HEAD>
<TITLE>Jumps</TITLE>
</HEAD>
<BODY BGCOLOR = FFFFFF TEXT = 000000>
```
                                        "top" jump point
```
<H1> <A NAME = "top"> Welcome </A> </H1>


<HR>                           Jump to "me"
<H2>Contents </H2>
<H3><A HREF = "#me"> This is Me </A>
<BR><A HREF = "#my job"> My Job </A>
<BR>The Cleethorpes Surfing Club    Jump to "my job"
<BR>My Cat's home page
```
                                    "me" jump point
```
<HR>
<H2> <A NAME = "me"> All about me </A> </H2>
What a fascinating chap I am...(more lies...)
<P>                               Jump back to "top"
<A HREF = "#top"> Return to the top </A>
```

"my job" jump point

```
<HR>
<A NAME = "my job"> <H2> My Job </H2> </A>
```

I'm a Careers Adviser, and let me give you some advice -
don't choose this as a career. <P>

```
<A HREF = "#top"> Return to the top </A>

</BODY>
```

Jump back to "top"

```
</HTML>
```

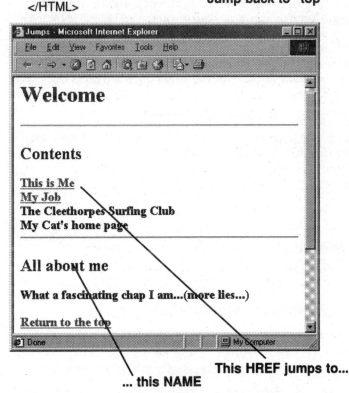

... this NAME

This HREF jumps to...

Reaching other directories

Keeping everything in the same directory is always the simplest solution, but if you have to reference pages, graphics or
any other files in other directories, here are the rules.

If the file is in a sub-directory of the one holding the page that
calls for it, use the pattern *directory_name/filename*:

```
<A HREF = "holiday/snapbook.htm">
```

finds the *snapbook.htm* page in the *holiday* sub-directory.

To get back up from a sub-directory, use double dots (..). e.g.

```
<A HREF = "../index.htm">
```

will take you back to the index page in the directory above.

If you need to refer to a file somewhere else on the system – not in the path above or below where the HREF is located – you will have to give the full path, from the root, down to the directory. Remember – the path starts with a forward slash, to specify the current system, and you must use a vertical bar line (|) and a slash, in place of the colon after the drive letter. For example:

```
<A HREF = "/C|/graphics/gallery.htm">
```

When you upload your files to your service provider, check first with them to find the correct path to your place in their system.

Tip

You can add *file://* before the link to define its type, but it works just as well – and sometimes better – without!

Jump points on other pages

If you want to be very precise in your linking to other pages, you can set up a link to a NAMEd jump point in another page.

```
<A HREF = "cats.htm#tiddles"> Go to Tiddles corner </A>
```

This will link to the *cats.htm* page, jumping to the *tiddles* part of it.

Jump point references can be added to links to other pages elsewhere on the Web, as long as you know the NAME. This will jump-link to the updated links section of my *Teach Yourself HTML* page:

```
<A HREF = "homepages.tcp.co.uk/~macbride/tybooks#links">
```

…assuming that I haven't changed the page by then.

4.4 Links and images

Link tags do not have to be attached to text. You can anchor them to graphics, replacing the text with an <IMG SRC = ...> tag.

For example:

    <A HREF = www.MyFirm.com> <IMG SRC = logo.gif> </A>

That would create a link to your firm's home page (if it was called My Firm), based on the image of your logo. Look for the image link in this next example.

    <HTML>
    <HEAD><TITLE>Meggieland</TITLE></HEAD>
    <BODY>
    <H2>Welcome to Cleethorpes</H2>
    <A HREF = meggies.html> <IMG SRC = meggies.gif></A>
    <P><A HREF = surfsup.htm> Surfing the North Sea </A>
    <P><A HREF = tweet.htm> The Budgie-Fancier's Paradise</A>
    </BODY>
    </HTML>

A linked image is outlined in the same colour as the underlines of linked text.

An image certainly has more impact than text, but if your visitors choose not to download images, they will have nothing to see. The solution lies in the ALT option. This defines text to be displayed if images are not downloaded. The option is unusual in that you must put quotes around your text if you have more than one word. Miss them out, and only the first word will be displayed. If we edit the text to read:

```
<A HREF = meggies.html> <IMG SRC = meggies.gif ALT =
"How to get there"></A>
```

Then a text-only visitor will see this.

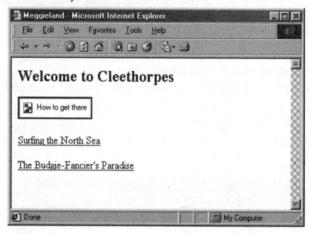

Tip

Attach an ALT option to any graphic, so that your visitors can tell what they will get before they download it.

```
<IMG SRC = beauty.gif ALT = "Picture of me, 389Kb">
```

At least they have been warned.

4.5 Multimedia links

You need a special reason for including multimedia clips in your pages. Audio and video compression techniques have improved no end in the last few years, but you still don't get much per megabyte. Depending upon the file format, the complexity of the image and the quality of the audio, 1 second of playing time can take anything from 20Kb to 200Kb – and even at the best, the images are fairly small and grainy. 1 megabyte of an audio/video file will give you between 5 and 50 seconds of playing time, but will typically take about 5 minutes to download. Any multimedia clip that you put on your page must be worth viewing – do you really expect your visitors to wait 5 minutes to hear you say 'hello and welcome to my site'? There can be good reasons for putting multimedia on your pages. You could put up clips of baby's first steps, or highlights of the office party, as a way of sharing the moments with friends and family. If you are in the video or music business, you could use the site to offer demos. If people want to see or hear the clips, they will be prepared to wait for files to download.

If you intend to use clips, do check that your service provider allows you enough Web storage space. Some of the less generous providers restrict their users to as little as 1Mb of space, which will not go far if you are into multimedia.

Remember that your visitors will only be able to view them if they have the right software. AVI and WAV files should present few problems for most visitors, as these can be handled by the standard Windows 95/98 Media Player. In XP, Media Player can also handle the newer and more efficient WMA and WMV formats. If you are using other file types, then it might be an idea if you also included a link to an FTP site where your visitors could find the necessary viewing software.

Multimedia files are pulled into a page with the HREF link.

```
<A HREF = "newwave.avi">
New video from the hottest rock group in Neasden (959Kb)
</A>
```

```
<A HREF = "jo walks.wmv"> Jo's first steps (725Kb) </A>
```

Do include the file size in the accompanying text.

```
<HTML>
<BODY>
<P><A HREF="newstar.wav">Hear the hottest new voice on the Web (2.4Mb)</A></P>
</BODY>
</HTML>
```

4.6 Links off the Web

HTML links are not restricted to local files and pages on the World Wide Web. You can also create links to other parts of the Internet. Two types of links are particularly worth noting.

FTP

FTP is the Internet's standard File Transfer Protocol. It defines the way that files are transferred over the Internet. FTP sites are host computers with (some) directories open to the public, and suitable software to enable users to download files from – and upload them to – these directories. Browsers have limited FTP capabilities built into them, so that they can download from FTP sites. If you want to upload, you need WS_FTP (see the next chapter). If you want to run an FTP site, you need another book!

You may have uploaded files, such as programs that you have written, pictures that you have created or whatever, to an FTP site, or found good software on an FTP site. If you want the world to know about them, and to be able to access them from your home page, you need a link like this:

```
<A HREF = ftp://kth.se/pub/tex/tools/pkzip/pkz204g.exe>
Download PKZIP (197Kb) </A>
```

Notice that the link starts with ftp://, so the browser knows how to handle it, and includes the site name and full path down to the file. The text should make it clear that the link will download a file, and – if possible – should give the file size.

If you just want to point people towards a good site, you can still use ftp://, but link to a site address, or a directory within it. The browser will display a directory listing when the link is used.

```
<A HREF =ftp://ftp.simtel.net/pub/simtelnet/>The public
directory at the SimTel.Net archives </A>
```

Updating links

If you include links to files and directories at FTP sites, revisit regularly to check that they are still there, and still in the same place. Nothing stays the same for long on the Internet!

E-mail

The *mailto:* facility gives a simple means for your visitors to contact you by e-mail. It will call up the mail creation window, with your address in the Mail To: slot, and will send the mail directly once it has been written.

<A HREF = mailto:jobloggs@yournet.co.uk> Mail me! </A>

Note: Do not start the URL with // if your mailbox is on the same server as your Web page.

Here are the new link types in use in a page:

```
<HTML>
<HEAD>
<TITLE>Links Off the Web</title>
</HEAD>

<BODY BGCOLOR=#FFFFFF>
<H3>Links elsewhere in the Internet</H3>
<P><A HREF=ftp://ftp3.ipswitch.com/Ipswitch/
Product_Downloads/ws_ftple.exe>Download WS_FTP
(690Kb) </A></P>

<P><A HREF=ftp://ftp.simtel.net/pub/simtelnet/>The public
directory at the SimTel.Net archives </A></P>

<P>Feedback:<A HREF=mailto:macbride@tcp.co.uk> Mail to
Mac </A></P>
</BODY>
</HTML>
```

Summary

◆ There are simple, standard rules that apply to HTML tags.

◆ The <A HREF = ...> tag set up a hypertext link to another page or file within your system or elsewhere on the Internet.

◆ When linking to other pages, use the http:// prefix. Always double-check the address after you have typed it – they are easy to get wrong!

◆ Using <A NAME = ...> you can mark a point within a document, that can be jumped to. The incoming jump can originate within the same document, or from elsewhere on the Web.

◆ The start point for a hypertext link can be an item of text or an image – or both.

◆ When using an image as a link, you should include ALT text for visitors who do not download the graphics automatically.

◆ Links to multimedia files use the same <A HREF = ...> tag.

◆ If you want to include multimedia files in your pages, do check that your service provider will allow you enough storage space for them.

◆ If you have a set of linked pages, or are using images and other files in your pages, you will save yourself trouble if you keep all your files in the same directory.

◆ Using FTP:// you can link directly to files in FTP sites.

◆ The MAILTO: link allows visitors to send e-mail to you easily.

05

onto the web

In this unit you will learn

- how to organize your pages ready for publishing
- how to upload your pages
- how to let people know about your site

5.1 Getting ready

Your files

When your page(s) and images are uploaded to your service provider's computer, they will normally all be stored in one folder. (You may be able to create subfolders within your part of their system, but that creates complexities you do not need.) Set up a new folder on your own system and copy into it the HTML documents and graphics files that make up your home page set. Having everything you need in one place – a place that is not cluttered up with unwanted files – will make life easier when you upload.

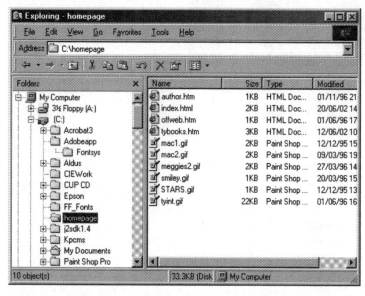

Get all the pages and graphics together in a special folder.

Final test

Run your browser, turn off the image loading and open your home page file. How does it look as a text-only page? If you have several linked pages, use the links to check out each one. Can you move between all the pages? Do they all look OK in text-only mode?

Work through the pages again, downloading the images as you go. Are all the images displayed correctly? Are you happy with the layout? If you have any design changes to make, now is the time to do it. (Though you can edit and upload new versions of your pages – or add more, delete or replace the lot – at any point in the future.)

Your service provider

Before you can upload to your service provider, you need to know where to put your files, how to get them there, and what to call your home page – the top one of the set – when it is on site.

At most Internet service providers the home page must be called *index.html* (note the 'L' at the end). The fact that every user's home page has the same name is irrelevant, as each is in its own folder, and will be identified by its path. Exactly where your files will be stored is generally irrelevant. They will normally be somewhere on an FTP server, and when you log in to that server, it will take you directly to your directory.

Read their documentation, read their on-line help service (if any) and if that still doesn't tell you what you need to know, ring up and ask.

HTM and HTML

On the Unix systems that most service providers use, HTML documents are identified by the extension .HTML. On a PC, they are normally identified by the extension .HTM, though Windows permits the use of .HTML.

Your service provider, like my local one at TCP, may insist that the home page document has an .HTML name, though subsidiary pages can have the .HTM extension. If this is the case, go through your pages now and edit any links back to the home page to add 'L' to the end of the name. If necessary, you can change the home page's name after you have uploaded it.

5.2 WS_FTP

This is the standard Windows application for handling your end of an FTP connection. If you do not have a copy, get one now. You can download it through your browser from the home site of its author (John Junod), at:

> www.ipswitch.com

The FTP connection

If you have used FTP before, it will probably have been to connect to one of the public FTP sites. With these, you log in as Anonymous, giving your e-mail name as a password. (WS_FTP will have collected this from you during installation, so you won't need to enter it for each new site.) Once at an FTP site you have limited access – downloading from public directories and uploading to designated incoming ones. You cannot normally create directories or rename or delete files. Logging in to your own directory on your provider's system is a different matter, as this is *your* place. You – and only you – have control here.

Directories and folders

On Web servers folders are called directories. In fact, this is what they were called on all computers before Microsoft decided that folders sounded better.

Accessing your Web space

Log in to your service, then run WS_FTP. It should start with the Session Profile panel open. If it is not open, click on the **Connect** button to open it.

Click **New**, then type in a **Profile name** for the connection – this can be anything that is meaningful to you.

For the **Host name**, enter the name of your provider's FTP server. The **User ID** and **Password** are the same as the ones that you use to get online with your browser. If no one else has access to your PC, tick **Save Pwd** so that you don't need to enter it in future.

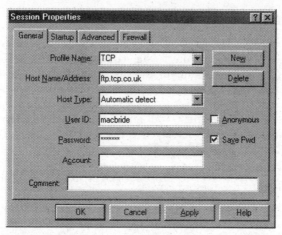

If your PC is secure, tick **Save Pwd** so that you don't have to type it in every time.

You can change directory after you have logged in, but it is quicker and simpler to do it now. Switch to the **Startup** tab. If you have been given the path to your directory at the service provider, enter it into the **Initial Remote Host Directory** slot. (Don't worry if you haven't been told – it almost certainly means you don't need to know.) Enter the path to the home page files' directory in the **Initial Local Directory** slot.

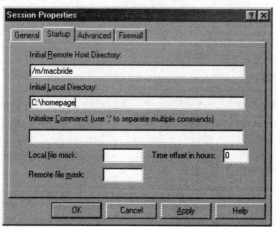

Click **OK** to move to the main screen. You are ready to upload.

5.3 Uploading

If everything is set up correctly, you should see a succession of messages scrolling through the narrow bottom pane of the WS_FTP window. Though some may be cryptic, and others move off before you have had a chance to read them, you should see enough to know that the conection is being made. You will know that you are there and ready to upload when you see your directory's name displayed at the *Remote System* slot at the top right of the window, and other activity ceases.

Select the files in your home page directory, and click 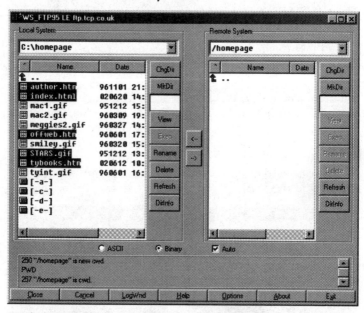 to send them to the remote system.

With larger files, you will see a Transfer Status panel open, displaying the progress of the uploading. HTML files are normally so small and transfer so quickly that all you see is a flash on the screen.

The whole set shouldn't take more than a few minutes to upload. After the last one has gone in, the directory listing on the Remote System pane will update. Check that they are all there, and if they are, click **Close** to shut down the FTP connection and click **Exit** to close WS_FTP.

5.4 Web Publishing Wizard

Windows users can upload their files with Microsoft's Web Publishing Wizard. It's usually included in the Windows suite or in Internet Explorer update packages, but if you haven't got a copy, you can download one from Microsoft's site.

There are several ways to use the Wizard. This is probably the simplest way.

Locate all the files that you want to upload, and place them in a folder by themselves – if necessary make a new folder to hold them.

Contact your Internet Service Provider and find the URL of your Web space – this may be either an http:// or an ftp:// URL.

You are now ready to run the Wizard.

The first time that you use the Wizard, you will probably want to upload the whole set that makes up your home page system. Later, you will normally only be uploading any new and edited files. Moving these into a separate folder will make uploading easier – you can simply send the whole folder.

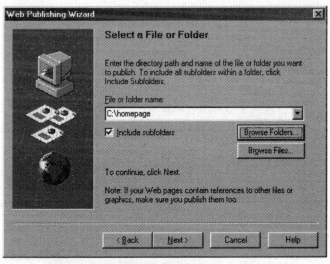

When the Wizard starts, the first job is to select the folder – click **Browse Folders** and locate your home page folder.

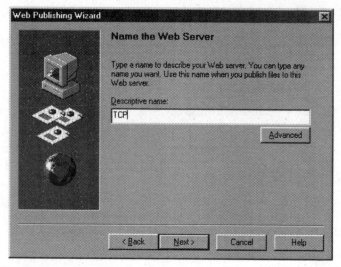

Give the server a name – any name will do as long as it means something to you.

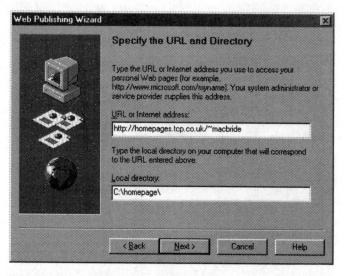

Enter the URL for your home page. The path to the local directory will have been copied in from the first stage of the Wizard. Notice that in the URL, a forward slash is used to separate the different parts of the address, but in the path to the local directory, you use a backslash.

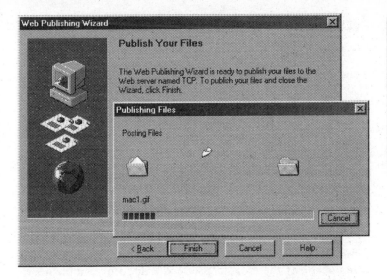

Click **Finish** to start uploading the pages. The Wizard will start up your dial-up connection, if necessary, then post the files, one by one, up to the server. Uploading is slower through the Web than using FTP, but it still shouldn't take very long.

5.5 Testing

Your home page should be accessible from the Web within a few minutes of uploading your files. If you haven't already found out your URL – you would have needed it if you had used the Web Publishing Wizard – go to your service provider's site, or ring them, now and find out.

Run your browser, get on-line and use the **File > Open** command to go to your home page. Can you get there? If not, it may be that their system is a little slow on recognizing the presence of new home page files.

Does it look as good on-line as it did during testing? Do the images download at a reasonable speed? Do the links all work? Remember that now you can test the links to other people's pages, FTP files, etc., as well as the links between your own pages.

Is it back to the drawing board, or is it time to let other people know that you are there?

5.6 Publicity for your page

The key question here is 'Who do you want to visit you?'

If the aim is to make this a place for family and friends to drop in to pick up your latest news, then the best way to publicise your page is to ring them up and tell them that it's there.

If you have assembled links and information about your hobby or special interest, and would like to share this with fellow enthusiasts, then post an article in the relevant newsgroups announcing your arrival on the scene (and hit the directories – see below).

If yours is a business home page, there may still be relevant newsgroups where an announcement would be welcomed, but this must be done thoughtfully. Some groups are distinctly non-commercial and do not appreciate business advertising – an announcement there could produce a flood of complaints in your e-mail. Some groups accept – and some are designed for – business home page announcements. Don't post to groups you don't know. Join and read enough of the articles in a newsgroup to get its flavour before you post to it.

If you are running an enthusiasts' resource page or a business page, or if you are a plain old-fashioned extrovert, *hit the directories*. There are several hundred directories on the Internet – large and small, specialised and general. Get your page into some or all of those and you should have visitors.

You can submit your page's URL to individual directories. The best way to do this is to go to the directory and look for a *Submit* sign. If you don't see one, they probably don't take un-solicited links. Amongst others, you might like to try:

Yahoo (www.yahoo.com),

Excite (www.excite.com/directory)

Lycos (http://www.lycos.co.uk/service/addasite.html)

The second approach is to use a site promotion service such as AddMe (www.addme.com). They will take your URL and details of your pages and submit them to the Web directories and search engines. AddMe offer a free service, which will get you into Lycos, Google, Excite and a dozen or so other major sites. They also offer a professional service which will promote your site much more widely and give you analysis and feedback.

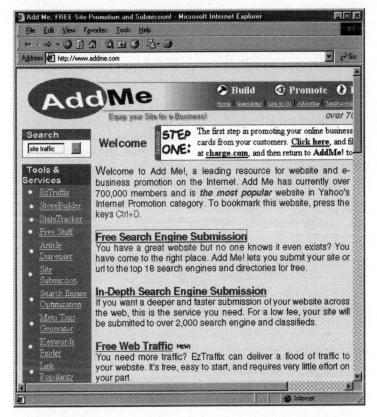

AddMe offers a one-stop approach to advertising your pages on the Web. If you want to get known, but don't have the time or energy to chase around the directories and search engines yourself, a promotion service is the answer.

5.7 META and ISINDEX

<META>

<META > tags go into the <HEAD> area, and are not visible on the page. They are mainly used to carry information about the page and its author. The basic shape is:

```
<META NAME = ... VALUE = ...>
```

The NAME identifies the nature of the information, and the information itself is the VALUE. For example:

    <META NAME = author VALUE = "Ingrid Bottomlow">

If the VALUE contains more than one word, they should be enclosed in "quotes".

An important use for <META> tags – and why I have introduced them at this stage – is for carrying keywords. Some of the Internet's search engines will look for these and use them when compiling their databases. The tags should follow the pattern:

    <META NAME = keyword VALUE = "..." >

Keywords are not special words, simply ones that indicate the contents of your page. For example, the Cleethorpes Surfing Club home page might use this keyword tag:

    <META NAME = keyword VALUE = "surfing, water sports,
    North Sea, frostbite" >

<ISINDEX>

This provides another way to define words or phrases to be picked up by the search engines. Use it in the form:

    <ISINDEX PROMPT="Keywords">

The keywords are used in the same way as in the META tags.

5.8 Counters

If you want to know how many people have visited your page, you can install a counter. For this you need a little help. You cannot actually count the number of visitors to your home page yourself, but there are a number of organizations on the Web that can do the counting for you. Their services are usually free – it is something they do to advertise their Web presence.

I got my counter from Net Digits, at:

    http://www.digits.com

Contact them when you have got your home page up and running successfully. There is a form to fill in, to give them the details of your page, and to set up your counter at their site.

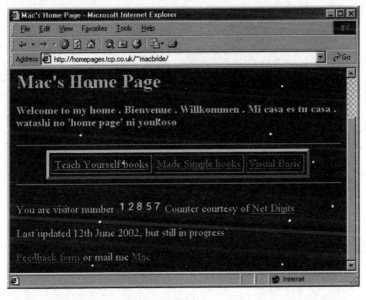

Come and see me – if only to boost my counter score!

The counter is given a name, which can be anything you like, e.g. 'maccount'. Once it has been created and its name confirmed, you can write a link to it into your home page.

The link is written into an <IMG SRC ...> tag, and should look something like this:

    <IMG SRC = "http://counter.digits.com/wc/maccount">

Obviously, the URL will depend upon the counter service you use and the name you choose.

The counter can be embedded in some text:

    You are visitor no. <IMG SRC = "http://counter.digits.com/wc/
    maccount"> since 21st October 1997

Other organizations offering free counters include, GoStats at:

    http://gostats.com/counter.html

and Microsoft's bCentral at:

    http://www.bcentral.com

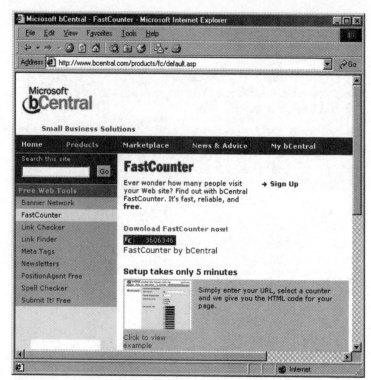

bCentral offers a number of Web promotional services as well as the free counters. If you are thinking about doing business over the Web, visit bCentral and see how they can help.

Summary

◆ When preparing to upload, start by organizing your HTML documents, graphics and any other related files into a single folder on your system.

◆ Test your system thoroughly before uploading – and pay special attention to the links between its pages.

◆ To upload your files to your service provider's computer, you will probably need WS_FTP.

◆ Microsoft's Web Publishing Wizard is easier to use than FTP, though uploading takes a bit longer.

◆ Once your Web page is in place, test it thoroughly, trying out every link.

◆ If a directory site has a 'Submit your URL' (or similar) message, you can publicize your page there.

◆ If you go to AddMe you can add your page to many directories and search engines.

◆ Keywords can be written into <META> and <ISINDEX> tags for the Internet's search engines to pick up.

◆ You can add a counter to your page by setting one up at an access counter service, such as Net Digits or bCentral.

06

lists and lines

In this unit you will learn

- how to define lists
- how to change the bullet or numbering style
- how to draw lines

6.1 Bulleted lists

There are three types of lists – with bullets, with numbers or letters and lists of terms and definitions. For the first two types the techniques are the same, with the only difference being in the tags that define the list type.

A bulleted list is set up with the tag <UL> to mark its start and </UL> to close it.

Each item in the list is preceded by the tag <LI> (List Item). This needs no closing tag.

The default settings give you round bullets (●) but an option in the <UL> tag can be used to set a different bullet style.

For example:

```
<HTML>
<H4>Our Gold Star service includes</H4>
<UL>
    <LI>Free delivery
    <LI>No quibble 'Return if not delighted'
    <LI>Bio-degradable packaging
    <LI>Special 2 for the price of one offer on Garlic bread
</UL>
</HTML>
```

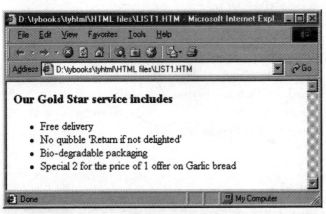

These items will all fit on single lines. If you have longer items, the continuation lines are indented to match.

Variations

You will see that with a plain <UL> tag, the bullets are filled circles. If you prefer, you can add the phrase "TYPE = *keyword*", where the keyword is either *square*, *disc* or *circle*.

square gives you a filled square;

disc produces a filled circle – the default bullet;

circle produces an open circle.

If you like, you can include sub-headings within a list. Simply set one of the <H...> tags – choosing an appropriate level. It will be displayed as usual, though indented.

```
<HTML>
<HEAD>
<TITLE>Bulleted lists</TITLE>
</HEAD>

<BODY>
<H3>Our Gold Star service includes</H3>
<UL TYPE = square>────────
<LI>Free delivery                    Bullet type
<LI>No quibble 'Return if not delighted'
<LI>Bio-degradable packaging
<LI>Special 2 for the price of one offer on Garlic bread

<H4>Toppings</H4> ──────────── Sub-heading

<LI>Pepperoni
<LI>Black Olives
<LI>Mushrooms                        More list items
<LI>Ham and Pineapple
</UL>
</BODY>
</HTML>
```

If you are subdividing your lists in this way, put extra blank lines into your code. They will make it easier to see the structure when you come back to edit it later.

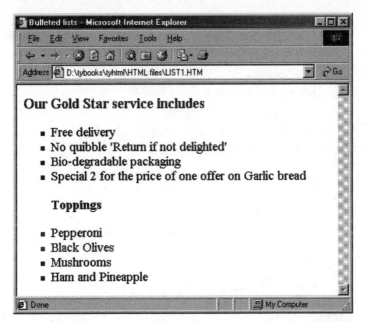

This is all one list. Notice that the 'Toppings' heading is indented to the same depth as the list items.

Nested lists

Lists can be 'nested', one inside the other, to give you several levels of indents. The same tags are used as for simple lists – but you must put a </UL> tag at the end of each inner level. Note that you can use different bullet styles for the inner and outer lists.

When writing nested lists, you will find it helpful to indent your inner list items in your code. It shows the structure more clearly, and it makes it easy to do a quick check that each opening <UL> tag has a matching </UL>.

Here are the 'Toppings' again, this time treated as a separate list, nested within the main Gold Star list:

```
<HTML>
<HEAD>
<TITLE>Bulleted lists</TITLE>
</HEAD>
```

```
<BODY>
<H3>Our Gold Star service includes</H3>
<UL TYPE = square>
<LI>Free delivery
<LI>No quibble 'Return if not delighted'
<LI>Bio-degradable packaging
<LI>Special 2 for the price of 1 offer on Garlic bread
<LI>With all your favourite toppings

    <UL TYPE = disc>
    <LI>Pepperoni
    <LI>Black Olives
    <LI>Mushrooms
    <LI>Ham and Pineapple
    </UL>

</UL>
</BODY>
</HTML>
```

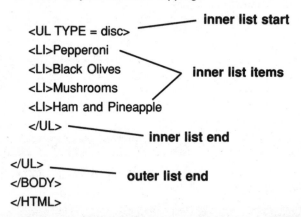

outer list start
inner list start
inner list items
inner list end
outer list end

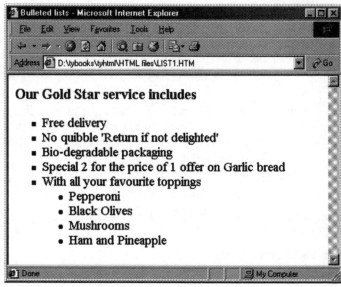

6.2 Numbered lists

Numbered lists follow exactly the same rules as bulleted lists, but here the tag is <OL>.

If you do not specify the TYPE, you get Arabic (normal) numbers, as in this example:

```
<HTML>
<BODY>
<H2>Top 5 Directories</H2>
<OL>
<LI><A HREF = http://www.yahoo.com>Browse at Yahoo</A>
<LI><A HREF = http://www.lycos.com>Browse at Lycos</A>
<LI><A HREF = http://www.google.com>Search at Google</A>
<LI><A HREF = http://www.altavista.com>Search at
AltaVista</A>
<LI><A HREF = http://www.ukdirectory.co.uk>UK Directory</A>
</BODY>
</OL>
</HTML>
```

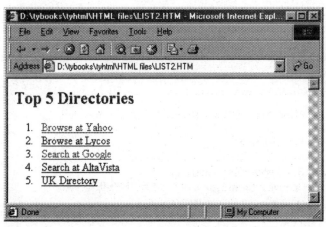

Plain Arabic numbers are the simplest to use, and can produce the clearest display.

If you want some variety – especially for nested lists – the TYPE options are 'I', 'i', 'A' and 'a'.

I   Roman capitals, I, II, III, IV
i   Roman numerals, i, ii, iii, iv
A   capital letters, A, B, C
a   lower-case letters a, b, c

Here's an example of nested lists, using several of the TYPE options. It's from our friend Ingrid, who is having a busy day.

```
<HTML>
<HEAD>
<TITLE>Numbered and nested lists</TITLE>
</HEAD>
<BODY>
<H2>Things to do</H2>
<OL TYPE = A>                          Level 1 list A,B,C
<LI>Clean out the Guinea Pigs
    <OL TYPE = I>                      Level 2 list, I, II, III
    <LI>Fetch the hay
    <LI>Push the pigs out of the way
    <LI>Shovel the old stuff where Pa won't fall in it
    </OL>                             End of level 2
<LI>Make some real bread
    <OL>                              Level 2 list, 1, 2, 3
    <LI>Buy some yeast
        <OL TYPE = i>                 Level 3 list, i, ii, iii
        <LI>Try the village shop
        <LI>Try Seamus Sosmall
        </OL>
                                      End of level 3
    <LI>Light the stove
    <LI>Get baking!
    </OL>
</OL>                                 End of level 2
</BODY>                End of level 1
</HTML>
```

Level 1 (A, B, C)

Level 2 (I, II, III)

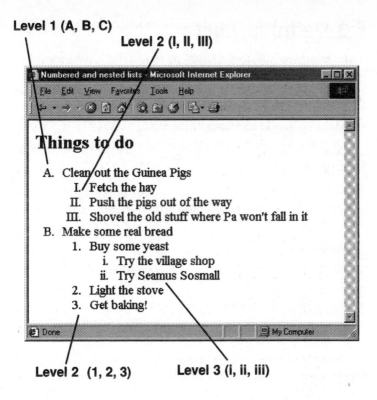

Level 2 (1, 2, 3)   **Level 3 (i, ii, iii)**

Combined styles

If you are nesting lists, you can use bullets for one level and numbers for another. A bulleted outer list and a numbered inner list can be a very effective combination.

Don't forget that you can change the FONT SIZE, or use <B>, <I> and other highlighting tags to make some levels of text more or less prominent.

6.3 Definition lists

These are ideally suited to lists of terms and definitions, but serve equally well for any set of text items where you want a series of sub-headings with following text. The tags used for these are:

<DL>	marks the start of the list
<DT>	identifies a term
<DD>	identifies the definition
</DL>	marks the end of the list

The <DL> and <DD> lines of text appear in the same font size and style – unless you specifically format them otherwise – but <DD> lines are indented one tab. The normal pattern is:

```
<DL>
      <DT>
            <DD>
      <DT>
            <DD>
      ...
</DL>
```

But there is nothing to stop you having several <DT> or <DD> tags in succession if you have a number of terms without definitions or several paragraphs of definition to one term. You can see this in the next example.

Special characters

The symbols '<' (less than), '>' (greater than), '&' (ampersand) and '"' (quote) have special meanings in HTML. If you want to use them in your text, you must substitute these expressions:

<	&lt (Less Than)	>	&gt (Greater Than)
&	&amp	"	&quot

Look out for them in the next example.

```
<HTML>
<HEAD>
<TITLE> Definition Lists </TITLE>
</HEAD>
```

```
<BODY>
<H2> List tags </H2>
<DL>
    <DT> &lt UL TYPE = square/disc/circle &gt
    <DD> Marks the start of an Unordered (bulleted) list
    <DT> &lt OL TYPE = i/I/a/A &gt
    <DD> Marks the start of an Ordered (numbered) list
    <DT> &lt DL &gt
    <DD> Marks the start of a Definition list.
    <DD> This takes no options
    <DT> &lt LI &gt                      <DD> for second definition
    <DT> &lt /DL &gt
</DL>                                     2 <DT>s without definitions
</BODY>
</HTML>
```

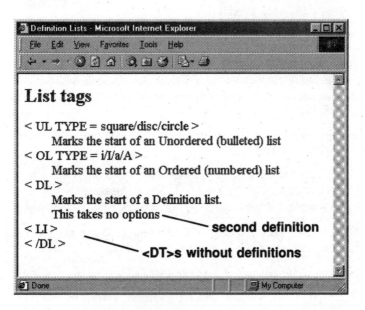

This definition list defines list tags! Notice how the '&lt' and '&gt' expressions have been displayed as symbols.

6.4 Fancy bullets

Bored with blobs in your lists? You can create fancy bulleted 'lists' by fitting your own bullet images at the starts of lines. These won't be proper lists, as defined by <OL> or <UL> tags, but they will look good on screen. It is more work, as you have to make the bullets and set the indents – which is, in effect, what the list tags do for you – but the results are worthwhile.

Create the bullet image in Paint. If your drawing skills are not too hot, then use a Wingding character – 24 point is a good size. Select the image, and use **Edit|Copy To...** to save it to file. Use Lview or PaintShop to convert this to a GIF file, and save it in your HTML directory.

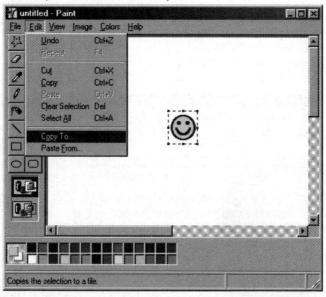

Here I have used Wingding 'J' for the image. At this point, it has just been selected and is about to be saved as a BMP file.

Now to build the list. There are three things to bear in mind:

● We need an image at the start of every item line.

● To create an indent, we will need to set the HSPACE value in the <IMG SRC ...> tag.

● The lines of item text must be separated – and <BR> will give a shallower break than <P>.

The resulting source code is nothing like as compact as an <OL> or <UL> list, but the display is better.

In this example, I have also replaced the top heading with a graphic.

```
<HTML>
<BODY>
<CENTER>
<IMG SRC = top5head.gif ALT = Top 5 Directories>
</CENTER>
<P>
<IMG SRC = redbtn.gif ALIGN = TOP HSPACE = 20><A
HREF = http://www.yahoo.com>Browse at Yahoo</A>
<BR>
<IMG SRC = redbtn.gif ALIGN = TOP HSPACE = 20><A
HREF = http://www.lycos.com>Browse at Lycos</A>
<BR>
<IMG SRC = redbtn.gif ALIGN = TOP HSPACE = 20><A
HREF = http://www.google.com>Search at Google</A>
<BR>
```

HSPACE to indent the text

Use <P> for deeper spacing

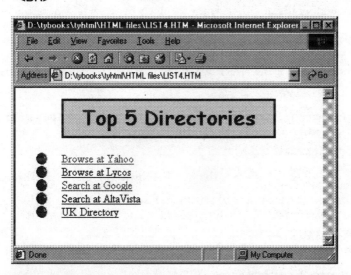

Bullets are usually very small files – under 1Kb – and so will download quickly.

```
<IMG SRC = redbtn.gif ALIGN = TOP HSPACE = 20>  <A
HREF = http://www.altavista.com>Search at AltaVista</A>
<BR>
<IMG SRC = "redbtn.gif" ALIGN = TOP HSPACE = 20><A
HREF = "http://www.ukdirectory.co.uk">UK Directory</A>
</BODY>
</HTML>
```

6.5 Line styles

The basic <HR> line is two pixels deep, stretches more or less the full width of the window, and has a shaded effect. These aspects can all be changed by options in the <HR> tag.

SIZE = *value*

This sets the thickness of the line, counting in pixels. The SIZE must be at least 2 if you want a shade effect. Over about 8 pixels, it looks less like a line than a box.

WIDTH = *value*

This sets the width of the line. As with the WIDTH option of images, you can either count in pixels or set it to a percentage of the browser window's width. Unless you want the line to match a heading or image, or you are creating a pattern of lines, it is usually best to set the width as a percentage. You then get the same effect, whatever size window it is viewed in.

ALIGN = *value*

This sets the line to the left, right or in the centre of the screen. It can only be used if the width has been set.

NOSHADE

If this keyword is used, the line is shown as a plain dark line.

You can see the effect of setting the SIZE and (pixel) WIDTH in this example. Try it for yourself – and with other values.

```
<HTML>
<BODY>
<H2> Horizontal Rules </H2>
```

```
<H3>Changing the Size</H3>
<HR SIZE = 1>
<HR SIZE = 2>
<HR SIZE = 4>
<HR SIZE = 6>
<HR SIZE = 10>

<H3>Setting the Width</H3>
<HR WIDTH = 50>
<HR WIDTH = 100>
<HR WIDTH = 200>
<HR WIDTH = 400>
</BODY>
</HTML>
```

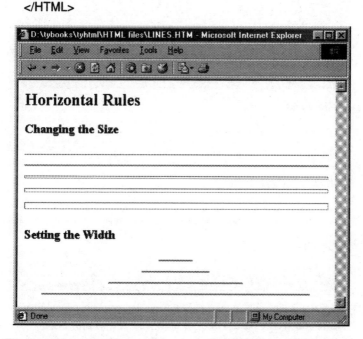

The first line in the Size set is only 1 pixel deep – note that it is not shaded. In the Width set, the first two lines are too small to be significant if used alone, but can be combined with longer lines to good effect.

This next example brings in the ALIGN and NOSHADE keywords, sets WIDTH in percentages and also applies several settings to some lines.

```
<HTML>
<BODY>
<H3>Alignment</H3>
<HR WIDTH = 40% ALIGN = left>
<HR SIZE = 6 WIDTH = 60% ALIGN = center>
<HR WIDTH = 40% ALIGN = right>

<H3>Shade or NOSHADE</H3>
<HR SIZE = 4 WIDTH = 80%>
<HR SIZE = 4 WIDTH = 80% NOSHADE>
</BODY>
</HTML>
```

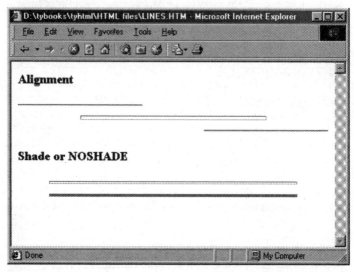

I don't know about you, but I prefer the standard 3-D shaded lines to the NOSHADE effect. I think we'll forget that option.

6.6 Graphic lines

For a really different divider, create a slim graphic, and place that in your document instead of an <HR> line.

Set the image in <CENTER> tags, and use <P> either side for good spacing from the surrounding text. For example:

```
<P> <CENTER><IMG SRC = "lineimg.gif"> </CENTER> <P>
```

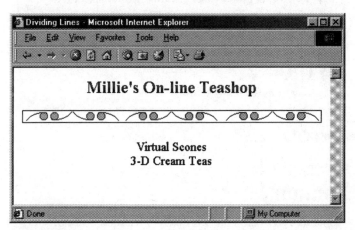

Add a little style to your page with a tasteful decorated divider! This one was created in Paint, but DTP packages can be a good source of decorated lines if you do not want to make your own.

You can also use an image to create vertical lines in the background – a thickish bar of contrasting colour down the left edge can be very effective. The image does not need to be a large one. As HTML automatically repeats any background image to fill the screen, all that is essential is that the graphic is too wide to be repeated across the screen.

Something like this, for example, will fit the bill nicely. It is 800 pixels wide, so cannot be repeated across even the widest screens, but only 25 pixels deep – and could be even less. The file is fractionally over 1Kb, and so will download in a fraction of a second.

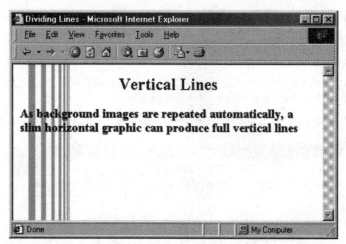

Vertical lines can make an effective background. The image is less than 1Kb – adding little to downloading time.

Summary

◆ Sets of short items can be neatly presented as lists.

◆ Lists can be nested inside one another, and headings can be used within lists.

◆ The <UL> tag creates bulleted lists. Its TYPE option gives you a limited choice of bullet styles.

◆ Ordered lists, set up with the <OL> tag, can have Roman or Arabic numbers or lower-case or capital letters.

◆ Definition lists were designed for terms and definitions, but suit any data where a sub-heading is to be followed by plain text.

◆ You can inset images into lists, to act as bullets.

◆ The <HR> tag can take several options to define the size and nature of the line.

◆ Images can be droppped into your page to act as dividers, in place of the <HR> lines.

07 forms

In this unit you will learn

- how to create simple forms for feedback
- how to add checkboxes, radio buttons and lists
- how to collect text inputs

7.1 The basic form

Unlike other aspects of HTML, forms involve two-way communication, and they will only function if your service provider is able to process the incoming data. This should not
create a problem – in essence all they have to do is run some
standard software to pick up the feedback from your visitors.
If your service provider cannot handle the feedback from forms,
give them a nudge.

A form can be written on a page of its own, or be included
within a larger page. It can include the normal range of text,
lists, images, links and other objects, but it can also include
the tags that will collect data and send the form.

The start of the form is marked by the <FORM> tag, and will
contain the two keywords METHOD and ACTION. These
can each take several options, and the simplest is this:

    <FORM METHOD = Post ACTION = mailto:your_address>

With these settings, the data entered into the form is e-mailed
to you when the form is submitted. Note that some older browsers cannot handle the **mailto** option. If you want feedback from
all your readers, you need to use a CGI script (see page 104).

Within the form, data is collected mainly in <INPUT ...> tags.
There are a number of options that can be used here. The most
important is NAME = ... which sets up a *variable* – a place to
store data input by your visitor.

    <INPUT NAME = email>

This creates the variable *email.* It will be displayed on screen as
a blank data entry slot, 20 characters wide. For a different size
slot, add the option SIZE = ..., giving the number of characters.

Put some text nearby, so your visitors know what it is for:

    E-mail address: <INPUT NAME = email SIZE = 30>

A second option that you must know about is one that sets up
a button to send the form's contents back to you. The basic
shape:

    <INPUT TYPE = Submit VALUE = "Send Now">

The phrase:

> TYPE = Submit

defines it as a button that submits feedback. The similar phrase:

> TYPE = Reset

defines a button to clear the form's contents.

> VALUE = "Send Now"

defines the button's caption. You can use any text you like, but you must enclose it in quotes or only the first word will be displayed.

Using only what we have covered so far, we can produce this simple feedback form:

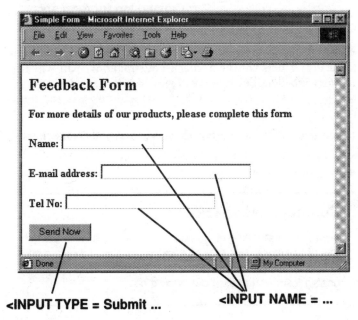

<INPUT TYPE = Submit ...   **<INPUT NAME = ...**

And here's the code that you need:

```
<HTML>
<HEAD>
<TITLE> Simple Form </TITLE>
</HEAD>
```

```
<BODY>
<H2> Feedback Form </H2>                          ———— Start of form
<FORM METHOD = Post ACTION = your_address>
<B>
For more details of our products, please complete this form <P>
Name: <INPUT NAME = Visitor> <P>
E-mail address: <INPUT NAME = Email SIZE = 30> <P>
Tel No: <INPUT NAME = Phone SIZE = 30> <P>
<INPUT TYPE = Submit VALUE = "Send Now">
</B>
</FORM> ——————
</BODY>                    ———— Closing tag for form area
</HTML>
```

When someone submits your form, it is mailed to you automatically. When you next check your mailbox, you will find
an entry labelled 'Form posted from Mozilla'. Read it, and you
will find an attachment. Look at that and you will see something like this:

Surname=Bill+Gates&Email=bgates@microsoft.com&Phone=...

Not the clearest way to present information, is it? We will look
at analysing returns on page 116.

Business feedback

If you are marketing a business on the Web, and expect
lots of feedback, talk to your service provider. Most can set
things up so that replies are collected, collated into a more
usable form and mailed out once a day.

7.2 Feedback from CGI scripts

We noted earlier that the ACTION = mailto: ... method does
not work with some older browsers. If you want to make sure
that all your visitors are able to mail the form, you need to use
a CGI script. And for this you need the co-operation of your
Internet service provider.

CGI is a programming language, devised for use on the Internet. Its scripts (programs) can only be run on suitable servers, such as the computers at your service provider. Most providers have several ready-made ones that you can use, and amongst these there should be one which will handle feedback from forms. The scripts are normally straightforward to use – a few adjustments to your form should be all that is needed.

Here is how you would use the feedback script at my service, Total Connectivity Providers. Theirs is the *formmail* script, by Matt Wright. Yours may use the same one, or something similar – but check with them before you go much further.

The <FORM ACTION... line calls up the script:

```
<FORM ACTION = "http://www.tcp.co.uk/cgi-bin/formmail"
METHOD = "POST">
```

Within the form, you must have a *recipient* field, which holds your e-mail address, so that the script knows where to mail the feedback. You don't want this to appear on the form, so it must be hidden. Here's what the line should look like:

```
<INPUT TYPE = "hidden" NAME = "recipient" VALUE =
"your_address">
```

Your form will almost certainly include fields for your visitor's e-mail address and real name. If you would like this information to be included in the From: line of the message, when the script mails it to you, those fields should be called *email* and *realname*.

```
<P>Name: <INPUT TYPE = text NAME = "realname">
<P>E-mail address:
<INPUT TYPE = text NAME = "email" SIZE = 30>
```

The rest of the form is identical, whether it is being returned to you by an ACTION=mailto: or by a CGI script.

Check the script

Do check with your service provider before starting on this. It is possible that they do not have a facility for running scripts, and even more likely that their scripts are used in a different way from the one described here.

7.3 Checkboxes and radios

If you want your form-fillers to be able to choose from a set of alternatives, you should use the TYPE options:

☑ Checkbox where several alternatives can be chosen, or

◉ Radio, where only one of the set can be selected

They are used in very similar ways, with one significant exception. With checkboxes, each INPUT should have its own NAME variable, to store the response.

```
I am interested in: <BR>
<INPUT TYPE = Checkbox NAME = hard> Hardware <BR>
<INPUT TYPE = Checkbox NAME = soft> Software <BR>
<INPUT TYPE = Checkbox NAME = books> Books <P>
```

If the visitor selects the *Hardware* checkbox, the variable *hard* will have the value *on*.

With radio buttons, the same NAME should be used for all the radios in the set, as you only want to allow one of the alternatives to be chosen:

```
Sex: <BR>
<INPUT TYPE = Radio NAME = sex VALUE = m CHECKED>
Male <BR>
<INPUT TYPE = Radio NAME = sex VALUE = f > Female <BR>
<INPUT TYPE = Radio NAME = sex VALUE = dk> Don't Know
<P>
```

We now need to add the VALUE = clause. This sets the value to be returned, so that the feedback will be in the form of *sex = dk* (if you have an indecisive visitor). If you omit the VALUE =, the feedback would read *sex = on*, whatever was selected.

Notice the keyword CHECKED in the first <INPUT...> above. This sets the default. Miss it out if you want to start with all the radios clear.

Compare this HTML code with the following screen display.

```
<HTML>
<HEAD>
<TITLE>Checkboxes and Radios</TITLE>
</HEAD>
```

```
<BODY>
<FORM METHOD = Post ACTION = mailto://
sales@clogs.com>
Tell me more about these wonderful Witherspoon clogs <P>
Style: <BR>
<INPUT TYPE = Checkbox NAME = trad> <BR>
<INPUT TYPE = Checkbox NAME = slipon><BR>
<INPUT TYPE = Checkbox NAME = gold> <P>
Sex: <BR>
<INPUT TYPE = Radio NAME = sex> <BR>
<INPUT TYPE = Radio NAME = sex CHECKED>  <P>
<INPUT TYPE = Submit VALUE = "Send">
<INPUT TYPE = Reset VALUE = "Clear and Restart">

</FORM>
</BODY>
</HTML>
```

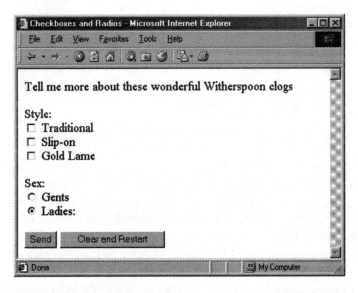

This form also has a TYPE = Reset button to clear the form, in case the visitor wants to start again.

7.4 Text areas

The simple <INPUT ...> only accepts one line of text. If you wanted to collect your visitor's (snail mail) address, you would have to use several of those, or one of these:

```
<TEXTAREA NAME = Address>
```

This displays as a small box with scroll bars to the right and bottom. It really is small. For most practical purposes you would want to make it into a decent size by adding the options ROWS and COLS to define the size of the display. The one in the screenshot below was produced by these lines:

```
Address: <BR>
<TEXTAREA NAME = Address ROWS = 4 COLS = 40>
</TEXTAREA>
```

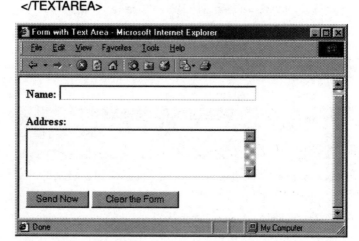

Three things to note here:

- The <BR> after the prompt text places it above the text area. If you miss this out, to put the prompt to the left, it aligns with the bottom of the text area and looks a mess.

- The ROWS and COLS settings only affect the display size. If your visitors want to write more lines, or longer ones, they can – that's what the scroll bars are there for.

- <TEXTAREA ...> needs a closing </TEXTAREA> tag.

7.5 Drop-down lists

Drop-down lists are one of the neatest ways of offering a set of alternatives. In HTML they can be implemented with the tags <SELECT ...> and <OPTION = ...>

<SELECT ...> provides the framework for the list. It takes the keyword NAME to define the variable where the selection will be recorded. The matching tag </SELECT> closes the list.

<OPTION = ...> defines an entry for the list. It must have a word in the tag – this will be fed back to you in the SELECT NAME variable – and a label to go on the list. You need an <OPTION = ...> tag for every item.

The tags fit together like this:

```
<SELECT NAME = Level>
    <OPTION = stand> Standard
    <OPTION = prof> Professional
</SELECT>
```

That gives us a drop-down list with two items.

If the visitor selects *Standard*, the *stand* option will be passed to *Level*, and the feedback mail will include this phrase:

```
Level = stand
```

An <OPTION = ...> tag can include the word SELECTED, to set that item as the default.

Look for the line:

```
<OPTION = Win SELECTED> PC/Windows
```

in this next example, and notice how the item *PC/Windows* is displayed at the top of the list, in the selection slot – though its natural place is further down.

```
<HTML>
<HEAD>
<TITLE>Drop-down Lists</TITLE>
</HEAD>
```

```
<BODY>
<H2> Order Form </H2>

<FORM METHOD = Post ACTION = mailto:sales@pcs.co.uk>
Order your software here: <P>
```
———— **Prompt**
```
Platform: <SELECT NAME = Platform>
   <OPTION = Pcdos > PC/DOS
   <OPTION = Mac> Mac
   <OPTION = Unix> Unix
   <OPTION = Win SELECTED> PC/Windows
</SELECT>

Level: <SELECT NAME = Level>
   <OPTION = stand> Standard
   <OPTION = prof> Professional
</SELECT>

<P>

<INPUT TYPE = Submit VALUE = "Send" >
</FORM>
</BODY>
</HTML>
```

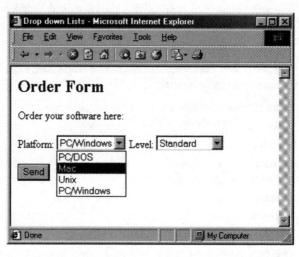

7.6 Prompts and labels

Never leave your visitors guessing. You should always include a prompt, even if you think that an option list should be self-explanatory. Your visitors can ignore prompts that they don't need, but they cannot read your mind. In the examples given in this chapter, the prompts are all very brief, and the forms would be more user-friendly if they had a little more in the way of helpful text.

<LABEL>

A <LABEL> can also act as a prompt. But this tag creates an active link with an <INPUT> field, so that selecting the label selects the field. This works with all <INPUT> types, but is most obvious – and most useful – with checkboxes and radio buttons.

```
<INPUT TYPE = Radio NAME = sex ID = male>

<LABEL FOR = male> Gents  </LABEL>
```

Notice that the <INPUT> tag has a new option ID = ... which is picked up by the FOR = ... option in the <LABEL>.

The <LABEL> looks like plain text – until you click on it, when it takes a dotted outline. Clicking a <LABEL> has the same effect as clicking its linked radio button or checkbox – it turns it on (or off if it was on already).

A <LABEL> can be written before or after its linked <INPUT>. Obviously, this changes the relative positions on the screen, but it doesn't make any difference to how it works.

Here's the checkboxes and radios example again, with the plain text prompt made into <LABEL>s.

```
<HTML>
<HEAD>
<TITLE>Labels</TITLE>
</HEAD>
<BODY>
<FORM METHOD = Post ACTION = mailto://sales@clogs.com>
Tell me more about these wonderful Witherspoon clogs <P>
```

Style: \
\<INPUT TYPE = Checkbox NAME = trad ID = trad>
\<LABEL FOR = trad> Traditional \</LABEL> \
\<INPUT TYPE = Checkbox NAME = slipon ID = slip>
\<LABEL FOR = slip> Slip-on \</LABEL>\
\<INPUT TYPE = Checkbox NAME = gold ID = gold>
\<LABEL FOR = gold> Gold Lame \</LABEL> \<P>
Sex: \
\<LABEL FOR = male> Gents \</LABEL>
\<INPUT TYPE = Radio NAME = sex ID = male> \
\<LABEL FOR = female> Ladies \</LABEL>
\<INPUT TYPE = Radio NAME = sex CHECKED ID = female>
\<P>
\<INPUT TYPE = Submit VALUE = "Send">
\<INPUT TYPE = Reset VALUE = "Clear and Restart">
\</FORM>
\</BODY>
\</HTML>

The only way that you can tell the difference between a plain text prompt and a \<LABEL> is by clicking on it.

7.7 Buttons

<BUTTON>

The <BUTTON> tag is a more flexible alternative to <INPUT TYPE = reset/submit> for creating clickable buttons. If all you want is a standard 'Submit', then it takes a little more work to do it this way, with no advantage. Compare these two lines. They produce identical results:

```
<BUTTON TYPE="submit"> Send me </BUTTON>    Send me
<INPUT TYPE = "submit" VALUE = Send me>      Send me
```

The point about the <BUTTON> tag is that you have more control over what appears on the button. You can format the text:

```
<BUTTON TYPE="submit"><FONT SIZE = 5 COLOR = red>
<B> Send me </B></FONT></BUTTON>
```

This gives you large, bold, red characters on the button.

You can even use an image instead of text...

```
<BUTTON TYPE="submit"> <IMG SRC = "sendme.gif">
</BUTTON>
```

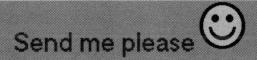

...or as well as text:

```
<BUTTON TYPE ="submit"> <FONT SIZE = 6> Send me
please</FONT> <img src = "smiley.gif"></BUTTON>
```

Submit image buttons

There is a special <INPUT TYPE = ...> option that is worth knowing about.

<INPUT TYPE = "image" SRC = "sendme.gif"> Send Me!

This displays the image, but makes it work as a submit button. The advantage of this is that it does not have the standard grey, rectangular background, which you get with <BUTTON>, but it can only be used for submitting forms.

7.8 A full featured form

Let's tie all these <INPUT ...> tags together in one form, then take a good look at the data that is returned from it.

The form (see the next page) includes a <TEXTAREA ...> for the visitor's address, checkboxes, radios and a <SELECT ...> list for their choices of options. Here's the code:

```
<HTML>
<HEAD>
<TITLE>Full Featured Form</TITLE>
</HEAD>


<BODY>
<FORM METHOD = Post ACTION = mailto://
    sales@artpaks.com>
<H2>On-Line Art Packs</H2>
Please send me information about your Art Collections
<P>
Name: <INPUT NAME = contact SIZE = 30> <BR>
Address: <BR>
<TEXTAREA NAME = Address ROWS = 4 COLS = 40>
</TEXTAREA> <BR>
Tel No: <INPUT NAME = Phone> <BR>
E-mail: <INPUT NAME = email SIZE = 30>
<P>
```

...continued on page 116

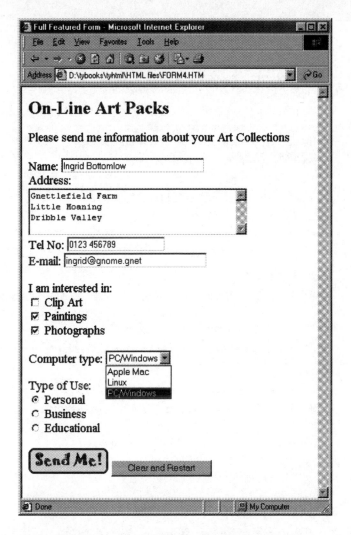

The form viewed on-line. Our visitor is in the process of selecting the computer type. Refer back to this when you get to the analysis in the next section.

I am interested in:
<INPUT TYPE = Checkbox NAME = clip> Clip Art
<INPUT TYPE = Checkbox NAME = paint> Paintings
<INPUT TYPE = Checkbox NAME = photo> Photographs
<P>

Computer type: <SELECT NAME = computer>
   <OPTION = Mac> Apple Mac
   <OPTION = Linux> Linux
   <OPTION = Win SELECTED> PC/Windows
</SELECT>
<P>

Type of Use:
<INPUT TYPE = Radio NAME = usage CHECKED> Personal

<INPUT TYPE = Radio NAME = usage> Business
<INPUT TYPE = Radio NAME = usage> Educational <P>

<INPUT TYPE = image SRC = "sendme.gif">
<INPUT TYPE = Reset VALUE = "Clear and Restart">
</FORM>
</BODY>
</HTML>

7.9 Analysing returns

If you get your form feedback from a CGI script, it will normally be in plain text or HTML format – ready to read. If it is sent back by a **mailto**, it will not be quite so readable.

Each of the NAME variables is followed by whatever your visitor typed in, though spaces will have been turned into '+' signs, and some symbols will have been replaced by code numbers – in this example '/' in 'PC/DOS' has become '%2F'. This is hexadecimal for 47, and the ASCII code number for '/'.

The variables are separated from each other by '&' signs.

Here's the feedback from Ingrid's visit to the last form:

```
contact=Ingrid+Bottomlow&Address=Gnettlefield+Farm%0D%0A
Little+Moaning%0D%0ADribble+Valley&Phone=0123+456789
&email=ingrid@gnome.gnet&paint=on&photo=on&computer=
Mac&usage=pers
```

It wouldn't take much to write a little program or a macro to convert this to a more usable form.

You could use a word-processor to make these these replacements:

Find	Replace with
&	new paragraph
%0D%0A	comma
+	space

It now reads:

```
contact=Ingrid Bottomlow
Address=Gnettlefield Farm, Little Moaning, Dribble Valley
Phone=0123 456789
email=ingrid@gnome.gnet
paint=on
photo=on
computer=Mac
usage=pers
```

From this, we can tell that Ms Bottomlow is interested in the Painting and Photograph collections (both set to *on*), but not Clip Art – if the variable is not *on*, it is not included in the feedback. She has also selected the *Mac* option from the *computer* list, and the *pers* radio button in the *usage* set.

Summary

◆ Forms are supported by all modern browsers, though if you wanted to guarantee that your visitors could get data to you, you should provide a simple e-mail alternative.

◆ At the start of every form, set the METHOD = to Post and give your e-mail address in the ACTION = option, to get feedback posted to you.

◆ CGI scripts will give more reliable feedback of form data. Your service provider should have ready-made scripts that you can use to get feedback.

◆ If an <INPUT ...> tag is to return a value, it must have a variable defined by NAME =.

◆ <INPUT TYPE = Checkbox> will create a tickable checkbox on screen. These can be used where multiple selections can be made.

◆ <INPUT TYPE = Radio> creates a radio button. Sets of radio buttons should share a NAME variable, but each have their own VALUE.

◆ For multi-line text data entry, use a <TEXTAREA ...> tag, setting the ROWS and COLS options if you want to fix their displayed size.

◆ Drop-down lists can be created with the <SELECT ...> and <OPTION ...> tags.

◆ The <LABEL> tag will link a prompt to an <INPUT> so that selecting the label selects the field.

◆ <BUTTON> is a more flexible alternative to <INPUT> for creating submit and reset buttons, allowing you to use formatted text and/or images on the buttons.

◆ The feedback from forms is not particularly easy to read, but a few minutes' search-and-replace in a word-processor will give you clear results.

08
tables

In this unit you will learn

- how to create simple tables
- how to add borders,
  headings and captions
- how to adjust the grid
- how to use tables for layout

8.1 The use of tables

Tables can be used to display text, links, graphics or any other items that can go anywhere else on a Web page. They may be any size from a couple of items in a single row, up to half a dozen or more columns and dozens of rows. They can be used simply as a means of presenting information, or can be so enhanced with borders, colours and graphics that they become decorative items in their own right.

8.2 The basic tags

For a simple table, you only need three pairs of tags, used in this pattern:

```
<TABLE>
<TR
    <TD> Column item </TD>
    <TD> Column item </TD>
    ... across the columns
</TR>

<TR>
    <TD> Column item  </TD>
    ... across the columns
</TR>
... down all the rows
</TABLE>
```

The table is built from the top left, working across the columns. Each item is enclosed in <TD> </TD> tags, and each row is enclosed in <TR> </TR> tags. It takes a lot of tags to make a big table!

Drawing up a rough sketch first helps to get the coding right. For instance, suppose we wanted a table of the Elements (the one that the old alchemists used, not the modern one – that's too big for us!). There are four elements. Here's our sketch:

Earth	Air
Fire	Water

The first row has two items – 'Earth' and 'Air', the second row has 'Fire' and 'Water'. That give us this HTML code:

```
<HTML>
<TABLE>
    <TR>
            <TD> Earth </TD>
            <TD> Air </TD>
    </TR>
    <TR>
            <TD> Fire </TD>
            <TD> Water </TD>
    </TR>
</TABLE>
</HTML>
```

Notice that I have indented each row by one tab space, and each item by a second. This is not essential, but it makes the document more readable and easier to check – you can simply run your finger down the page making sure than each <TR> has its matching </TR>.

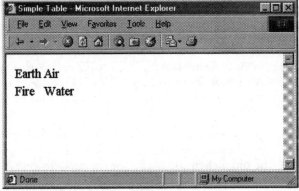

Not very impressive, but it's a start!

Let's try again. This time, we'll put two lines of text in each
<TD> place, setting the top line in <B> to make it into a header.

```
<HTML>
<HEAD>
<TITLE> Simple Table</TITLE>
</HEAD>
<BODY>
<TABLE>                                    First item
    <TR>
        <TD> <B>Word-processed documents</B> <BR>
        DOC, WPS, WP, RTF </TD>
        <TD> <B>Graphics Files</B> <BR>
        GIF, JPG, BMP, PCX, PCD, TIFF </TD>
    </TR>
    <TR>
        <TD> <B>Multimedia</B> <BR>
        AVI, WAV, MID, WMA, WMV </TD>
        <TD> <B>Executables</B> <BR>
        EXE, COM, DLL, VBX </TD>
    </TR>
</TABLE>
</BODY>
</HTML>
```

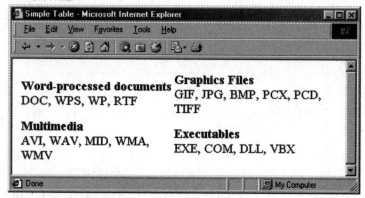

Where one item in a row takes fewer lines than another, it is set
in the middle of the vertical space.

8.3 Borders

Adding a border is very easy and greatly improves the look of tables. At the simplest, it is just a matter of including the keyword BORDER in the <TABLE> tag. Here is the same table with the tag edited to read:

    <TABLE BORDER>

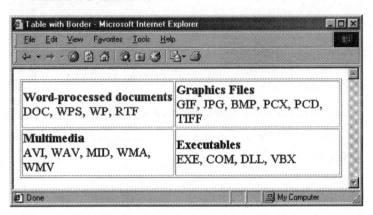

The default settings are to have each item bordered by a thin line, a slim border around the whole table, a narrow space between the inner and outer borders, and the text close to the edge of the inner borders.

The latter three settings can be changed.

BORDER can take a value, setting the thickness of the outer border. The value is given in pixels, e.g.:

    BORDER = 10

CELLSPACING = ... sets the distance, in pixels, around the border of each item.

CELLPADDING = ... sets the distance, in pixels, between the inner border and the text.

The options are all set in the <TABLE ...> tag:

<TABLE BORDER = 10 CELLSPACING = 10 CELLPADDING = 15>

Any of BORDER, CELLSPACING and CELLPADDING can be omitted – CELLSPACING and CELLPADDING are then set by default at 5 pixels.

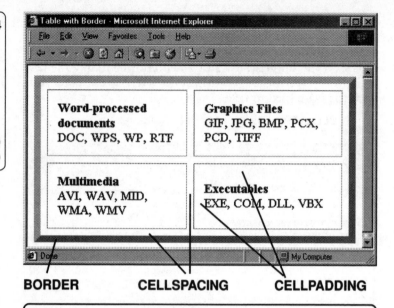

BORDER   **CELLSPACING**   **CELLPADDING**

Hiding inner borders

The border colours are set automatically to contrast with the background. However, if you set a BODY BGCOLOR value that uses only half-beam colours, e.g. "808000", "008000" or "808080", the inner borders disappear!

8.4 Headings and captions

Tables often need some headings to explain what they are about.

<CAPTION>

Use this to add a (bold) caption. It is normally placed above the table, but you can use the option *ALIGN = bottom* to place it below. The caption text must be closed with </CAPTION>.

<TH>

This marks a heading, to a row or column within the table. It is used like a <TD> tag, but sets the text in bold and aligns it in the centre of its cell. Close the heading with a </TH> tag.

This can take options to make the heading span more than one row or column. We will return to these on page 127.

As usual, it helps if you plan ahead. Here's a sketch of the table that I want to build.

blank cell

Caption

Up and Away Holidays

<TH>

<TH>

	Florida	**Malaga**	**Tuscany**
7 nights	£479	£399	£359
14 nights	£629	£519	£539

The table will have three rows and four columns. The top row will have four <TH> tags, including an empty one at the start to create that blank cell in the top left. The other two rows will each have one <TH> followed by three <TD> tags.

```
<HTML>
<HEAD>
<TITLE> Table with Headings</TITLE>
</HEAD>
<BODY>
<TABLE BORDER = 5 CELLSPACING = 5 CELLPADDING = 5>

<CAPTION>
<H3>Up and Away Holidays</H3> ———
</CAPTION>
    <TR>
        <TH> </TH> ———
        <TH> Florida </TH>
        <TH> Malaga </TH>
        <TH> Tuscany </TH>
    </TR>
```

Captions are normally in the standard font size

Blank cell

Column headers

```
        <TR>                                    Row header
            <TH> 7 nights </TH>
            <TD> £479 </TD>
            <TD> £399 </TD>
            <TD> £359 </TD>
        </TR>
        <TR>
            <TH> 14 nights </TH>
            <TD> £629 </TD>
            <TD> £519 </TD>
            <TD> £539 </TD>
        </TR>
    </TABLE>
    </BODY>
    </HTML>
```

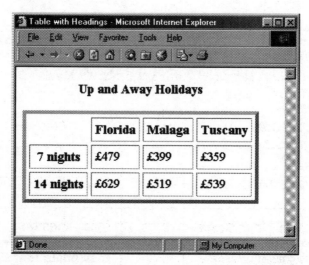

Note that the blank <TH> tag produces an unbordered space, rather than an empty cell. Setting the caption as an <H3> heading has forced a space beneath it. If we had used <FONT SIZE ...> to set the text size, it could have been kept closer to the table.

Fonts in tables

If you want to change the font of headings or entries in tables, you must write an <H ...> or <FONT SIZE ...> tag within the <TH> or <TD> tag for each item. You cannot set a size or style to apply to the whole table.

8.5 Irregular grids

Not all tables fit into a simple grid. With some you will want two or more levels of headings, with category headings in one row spanning a set of headings in the row below; an item within the table may apply to several rows and/or columns.

Both <TH> headings and <TD> items can be extended across or down the cells with the options:

ROWSPAN =   to set the number of rows deep

COLSPAN =   to set the number of columns across

Let's extend that last table, starting as before with a sketch.

Up and Away Holidays

		US	Europe	
		Florida	Malaga	Tuscany
7 nights	Full Board	£479	£399	£359
14 nights	Full Board	£629	£519	£539
	Self-Catering	£529	£419	

2 Rows x 2 Cols   2 Columns

2 Rows   2 Columns

The 'Europe' heading will be set up by:

```
<TH COLSPAN = 2> Europe </TH>
```

The 2 by 2 blank cell at the top left will be set up by:

```
<TH ROWSPAN = 2 COLSPAN = 2>  </TH>
```

The row after this one will only have three entries as the first column will already be occupied. Similarly in the bottom row, the previous row starts with the double-cell heading:

```
<TH ROWSPAN = 2> 14 nights </TH>
```

Look for these, and the other two multi-cell items in the full code for this table.

```
<HTML>
<HEAD>
<TITLE> Table with Headings</TITLE>
</HEAD>
<BODY>

<TABLE BORDER = 5 CELLSPACING = 5 CELLPADDING = 5>
<CAPTION>
<H3> Up and Away Holidays </H3>
</CAPTION>
    <TR>
            <TH ROWSPAN = 2 COLSPAN = 2> </TH>
            <TH> US </TH>
            <TH COLSPAN = 2> Europe </TH>
    </TR>
    <TR>
            <TH> Florida </TH>
            <TH> Malaga </TH>
            <TH> Tuscany </TH>
    </TR>
    <TR>
            <TH> 7 nights </TH>
            <TH> Full Board </TH>
            <TD> £479 </TD>
            <TD> £399 </TD>
            <TD> £359 </TD>
    </TR>
```

Only three items in this following row

```
        <TR>                              Double-depth heading
            <TH ROWSPAN = 2> 14 nights </TH>
            <TH> Full Board </TH>
            <TD> £629 </TD>
            <TD> £519 </TD>
            <TD> £539 </TD>
        </TR>
        <TR>                              Table entries are
                                          normally left-aligned
            <TH> Self-Catering </TH>
            <TD> £529 </TD>
            <TD COLSPAN = 2 ALIGN = Center> £419 </TD>
        </TR>
    </TABLE>
</BODY>
</HTML>
```

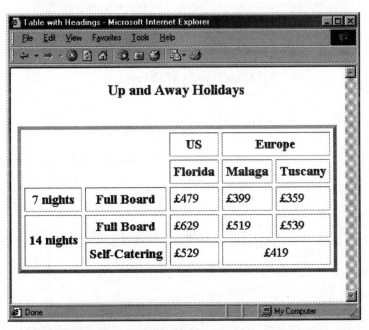

The displayed table, with headings and entries spanning across rows and down columns.

8.6 Alignment

You will have noticed in the last example that an ALIGN option was set for the last <TD...> item. Normally <TH> headings are aligned in the centre of their cells, both vertically and horizontally, and <TD> items are aligned to the left, in the middle of the space. If needed, these can be changed.

These options apply to both <TH> and <TD> tags.

ALIGN = can take the values *Left*, *Center*, or *Right* to set the horizontal alignment.

VALIGN = can take the values Top, Middle or Bottom to set the vertical alignment. These only have an effect if the row is deeper than the items.

Here's another version of the table, with alignments set for the top row.

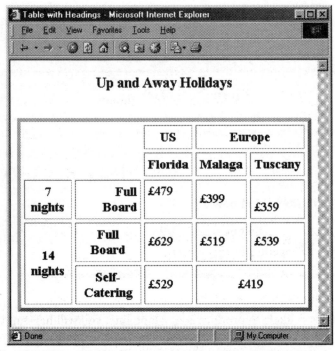

The VALIGN options only come into play if the table width is reduced so that the headings are forced onto two lines.

The relevant part of the code reads:

```
<TR>
        <TH> 7 nights </TH>
        <TH ALIGN = right> Full Board </TH>
        <TD VALIGN = Top> £479 </TD>
        <TD VALIGN = Middle> £399 </TD>
        <TD VALIGN = Bottom> £359 </TD>
</TR>
```

Varying displays

Tables adjust to fit the browser window. The row headings in the last screenshot have been wrapped onto two lines. With a wider window they would each have fitted on one line – and the vertical alignment effects would not have been visible in the narrow rows!

8.7 Images and links

Tables can hold any kind of items – not just text. If you intend exhibiting photographs or other artwork on your home page, it's a good idea to offer your visitors thumbnail previews. The six pictures in the next example occupy just over 20Kb in total as thumbnails – smaller than any individual picture at full size.

Thumbnails can be arranged conveniently in a table. Each can carry a link to a separate page with a full version of the picture. It is then up to your visitors whether or not they take the time to download them.

To set up a thumbnail table, each <TD> entry will need a link to its associated page, the image, and brief descriptive text. They fit together in this pattern:

```
<TD> <A HREF...> <IMG SRC ...> Text </A> </TD>
```

This makes both the picture and the text 'clickable'.

As this is likely to produce a very long line, you will have more readable code if you split it, at a convenient point, into two lines. You can see this in the example below.

```
<HTML>
<HEAD>
<TITLE> Thumbnail Table </TITLE>
</HEAD>
<BODY>

<TABLE>
<CAPTION> <H2> Views of the Dribble Valley </H2>
<CAPTION>
    <TR>
        <TD> <A HREF = bar.jpg> <IMG SRC = bar.gif>
        <BR>In the Green Gnome (26Kb)</A> </TD>
        <TD> <A HREF = bridge.jpg> <IMG SRC = bridge.gif>
        <BR>The Dribble bridge (28Kb)</A></TD>
    </TR>
    <TR>
        <TD> <A HREF = farm.jpg> <IMG SRC = farm.gif>
        <BR>Gnettlefield Farm (27Kb)</A> </TD>
        <TD> <A HREF = hill.jpg> <IMG SRC = hill.gif>
        <BR>Ploughgnome Lane (26Kb)</A> </TD>
    </TR>
    <TR>
        <TD> <A HREF = light.jpg> <IMG SRC = light.gif>
        <BR>Dribblemouth Light (28Kb)</A> </TD>
        <TD> <A HREF = mill.jpg> <IMG SRC = mill.gif>
        <BR>Uncle Dusty's Mill (25Kb)</A> </TD>
    </TR>
</TABLE>
</BODY>
</HTML>
```

Link — `bar.jpg`

Image — `bar.gif`

Text — `<TD> <A HREF = bar.jpg> <IMG SRC = bar.gif>`

Close link

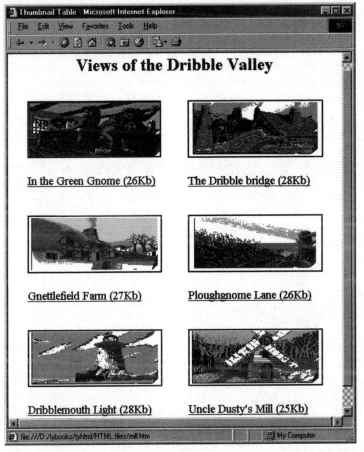

If the thumbnails are the same sizes, the text and images should line up evenly with those in other cells.

8.8 Tables and layouts

You saw that borders can be set to any size. If you drop the BORDER WIDTH down to 0, the borders disappear but the table is still there to provide a framework for holding images and text. We can use this to create newspaper style columns and other interesting layouts.

In the next example, the material has been arranged in three tables, rather than one. There are two reasons for this. It allows us to have different numbers of columns, and different widths, so we can allocate space as needed for the images and text at each point in the display. It also affects the way that the page downloads. A table has to be fully downloaded before it can be displayed – so large tables leave your visitors waiting for some little time. With several tables, your visitors can view the first while waiting for the others to come in.

Each table in this example is only one row deep. The one at the top has three columns, with an image in the centre. The other two each have two columns, with images in opposite sides.

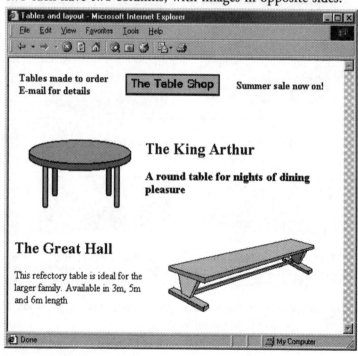

Here's the source code:

```
<HEAD>
    <TITLE>Tables and layout</TITLE>
</HEAD>
<BODY>
<TABLE BORDER =0 CELLSPACING=5>
<TR>
```

```
   <TD>
   <H4>Tables made to order<BR> E-mail for details</H4>
   </TD>
   <TD ALIGN = center>
   <H3><IMG SRC="TABLE1.gif" width = 80%></H3>
   </TD>
   <TD>
   <H4>Summer sale now on!</H4>
   </TD>
</TR>
</TABLE>
<P>
<TABLE BORDER=0 CELLSPACING=20 CELLPADDING=0>
<TR>
   <TD WIDTH="25%"><IMG SRC="TABLE2.gif"></TD>
   <TD>
   <H2>The King Arthur</H2>
   <H3>A round table for nights of dining pleasure</H3>
   </TD>
</TR>
</TABLE>
<P>
<TABLE BORDER =0 CELLSPACING=0 CELLPADDING=0>
<TR>
   <TD>
   <H2>The Great Hall</H2>
   This refectory table is ideal for the larger family. Available
   in 3m, 5m and 6m length</TD>
   <TD WIDTH = 60% ALIGN = center>
   <IMG SRC = "TABLE3.gif"> </TD>
   </TR>
</TABLE>
</BODY>
</HTML>
```

Summary

◆ Tables can be used to display text items, images or links.

◆ Tables are tag-intensive. Every data item must be enclosed in a pair of <TD> tags; every heading in <TH> tags; every row in <TR> tags.

◆ Borders can be added, and the thickness and spacing of their lines set by options.

◆ A caption can be placed above or below a table.

◆ Headings and data items can be spread across several columns, or down several rows if necessary.

◆ The text or image in a data cell or heading can be aligned vertically and horizontally.

◆ Tables are a good way of displaying thumbnail images if you are running an on-line 'gallery'.

◆ Tables allow you to lay out blocks of text alongside images – and if you set the BORDER width to 0, the frame will become invisible.

09

frames

In this unit you will learn

- how framed pages work
- how to create simple and nested framed pages
- how to display linked pages

9.1 The frame concept

With frames, you have two distinct types of document:

● *Layout documents* create the frames. They normally carry no displayed content whatsoever – their function is purely to divide the window up into areas.

● *Content documents* go into the frames. They are identical to normal pages, though you may need to adjust their links if the pages are to call each other up within the frame window. While you are experimenting, you can use any of your existing pages as content documents, without alteration. Later, you might want to edit and redesign them so that they work better in the new environment.

Fitting them together

A layout document can divide a window into any number of frames, either vertically or horizontally – but not both. However, a frame can hold another layout document, which can subdivide either vertically or horizontally. The nesting of frames within frames can go on ad infinitum, but in practice you wouldn't want to use more than two or three layout documents or more than three or four content frames in one page – it would just be too confusing for both you and your visitors.

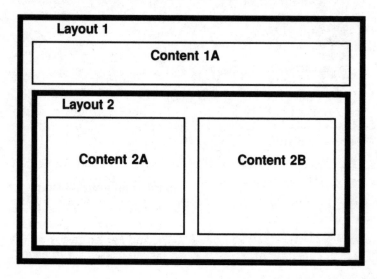

In the diagram, **Layout 1** contains two frames:

> **Content 1**
>
> **Layout 2**   containing two frames
>
> > **Content 2A**
> >
> > **Content 2B**

What's in the content documents is irrelevant at this stage – though crucial when you do it for real. A good way to use your frames is to have one that displays your logo, title or other identifier – this would stay on show permanently. A second frame will hold an index or contents list which allows your visitors to navigate through the set of pages that are displayed in the third frame. A large or complex site might have several contents lists which could be switched into the second frame to give access to different sets of pages.

The frame structure does not have to remain fixed. You can load a new layout document into a frame, or into the whole window, to give a different structure – and to link to new sets of contents documents.

9.2 Layout documents

There are three tags which apply only to layout documents – in fact, a layout document would normally only use these three, apart from <HTML> and <TITLE>.

<FRAMESET ROWS / COLS = value, value>

This defines the division of the window into frames. It can take either the ROWS or the COLS option – but not both – depending upon which way you want to divide. There is a *value* for every division.

The values can be given in three ways, and you would normally use two of these when defining the divisions:

Fixed define the width or depth of a frame in pixels:

    ROWS = 150, 300...

makes the first row 150 pixels deep, and the second row 300.

Percent sets the width or depth as a percentage of the browser window size:

    COLS = 25%, ...

makes the first column take 25% of the width of the frame.

Relative sets the width or depth as a fraction of the remaining area. The symbol '*' used by itself simply means all the rest of the space:

    ROWS = 200,*

sets up two frames, the first 200 pixels deep, the second taking up whatever space is left below.

* can also mean 'fraction', when used with a number.

    COLS = *, 3*

says, 'divide the window into two columns, with the second being 3 times as wide as the first'. It has the same effect as ...

    COLS = 25%, 75%

... but is quicker to write.

* is useful where you have a mix of fixed and percentage sizes:

    ROWS = 100, 25%, *

This creates three horizontal frames. The top one is 100 pixels deep, the second is 25% of the window height, and the third is whatever space is left.

</FRAMESET>

This closes the frame definition. Between <FRAMESET...> and this you define the contents of the frames using <FRAME ...>

<FRAME SRC = ... >

This is where you specify the document to be placed into the frame. Assuming that the document is another file in the same directory as the layout document, the tag might read:

    <FRAME SRC = banner.htm>

If the frame is to be used to display pages, which will be selected from a contents list in another frame, it will need a name:

    <FRAME SRC = toppage.htm NAME = showplace>

This frame will display the *toppage.htm* file when it first opens, then be used to display other pages that will be directed into it from elsewhere. We'll come back to this on page 144.

The tag can take some options to define the nature of the frame.

NORESIZE

fixes the size of the frame.

SCROLLING = Yes/No/Auto

forces scrollbars to be on (Yes), off (No), or leave it to the system to switch them on and off as necessary (Auto).

Let's put these together. The following code will only work properly if you have files called *banner.htm* and *inframe.htm*. Without them, you will get messages complaining about the missing files, but the frame structure will still be visible.

Fixed size frame at the top

```
<HTML>
<FRAMESET ROWS = 100,*>
  <FRAME SRC = banner.htm NORESIZE SCROLLING = No>
  <FRAME SRC = inframe.htm SCROLLING = Auto>
</FRAMESET>
</HTML>
```

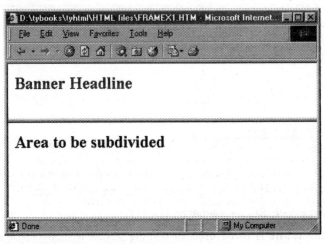

In this example, the *banner.htm* and *inframe.htm* files held simple headings, just so that something was visible.

If you wanted to keep things simple, you could stop at a two-frame display, putting a title graphic or text in the banner frame and your home page document in the main frame. Open the layout file in your browser, both contents documents should load in, and any pages linked from your top page should display in the main frame, when their links are activated.

But let's press on to create a two-layout, three-frame display. You need this second layout file, to be saved as *inframe.htm*.

```
<HTML>                              The left frame is narrow
<FRAMESET COLS = 30%,*>
  <FRAME SRC = navigate.htm>
  <FRAME SRC = content.htm NAME = contents>
</FRAMESET>
</HTML>
```

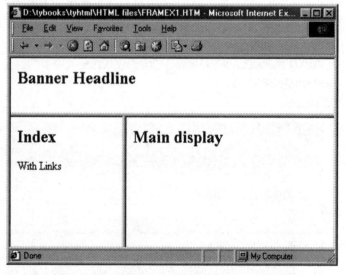

Here is the output, with temporary text in the *navigate.htm* and *content.htm* files. In the working version, *navigate.htm* would hold a set of links to act as an index to the pages, and *content.htm* would be the first page of the display.

<NOFRAMES>

Frames are not visible to any visitors running older browsers (Internet Explorer 3.0 or earlier). If you want to cater for them, the answer lies in the <NOFRAMES> pair of tags. These can be used, inside the <FRAMESET ...> tags, to enclose text and other material to be displayed on browsers that cannot handle frames. (The enclosed code is ignored by those that can.)

We can then set up a <NOFRAMES> section that gives a minimal welcome message and directs our visitors to the home page that would otherwise be reached through a link in the frames.

```
<HTML>

<FRAMESET ROWS = 100,*>

    <NOFRAMES>
    This page uses frames. <BR>
    Click <A HREF = index1.htm> here </A> for the
    no-frame version.
    </NOFRAMES>
... other frame stuff ...
</FRAMESET>

</HTML>
```

Viewed in an old browser, the frame page now looks like this:

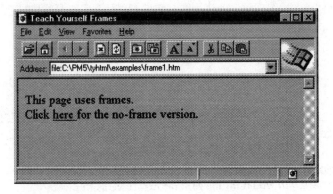

Frames and NoFrames

It can be tricky getting a site to look equally good in frame and no-frame versions. Stick to a fairly simple structure and you should be OK. In the frames, have an index frame to link to your other display pages, but put links in these so that it is possible to navigate through the pages without using the index frame. The links will be redundant in the frame version, but make the site workable to other people.

9.3 Links and targets

When you create a link to a page from a simple page, there is no question as to where the new page is displayed – it replaces the calling one. When you have frames, there is a question of where to display the linked page. The answer is supplied through an option in the <A HREF ...> tag.

<A HREF = "url" TARGET = ...>

Using frames, you have five alternative targets – places in which a linked page can be displayed.

TARGET =

framename displays in the frame identified as framename in its <FRAME SRC = ... NAME = framename> tag.

_self displays in the current frame. If you miss out the TARGET phrase, it has the same effect.

_parent replaces the layout document containing the linking frame, with the new page – which may well be a new layout document, giving a new structure.

_top replaces the top level layout document, i.e. the whole window, with the new page.

_blank opens a new copy of the browser and displays the page in there. You can have as many browser windows running at once as you like!

For example:

    <A HREF = myclub.htm TARGET = mainframe>

This displays the *myclub* page in the *mainframe* frame.

```
<A HREF = newframe.htm TARGET = _parent>
```

replaces the current layout document with the *newframe* one.

9.4 The framed home page

If you have followed the examples so far, you should now have the skeleton of a three-frame window. All it needs is some flesh.

The title frame

Design your own home page logo or graphic title, or create a strong, coloured text heading, to fit into the top frame. Save it as *banner.htm*. (If you have already got something suitable, change the SRC reference in the top level layout document.) The one used in the next screenshots looks like this:

```
<HTML>
<BODY>
<IMG SRC = tylogo.gif WIDTH = 100%>
</BODY>
</HTML>           Set the image to fill the frame
```

The index frame

The index, or contents list, frame – called *navigate.htm* in the earlier example – holds links to all the pages that you want to display. A <UL> list offers a neat way of presenting them.

At the simplest you can set the *contents* frame as the TARGET for them all, but experiment with the alternatives.

- If you use **TARGET** = **_self** (or miss out the TARGET phrase), the incoming document will overwrite your index. This will need a return link of the type:

  `<A HREF = navigate.htm> Return to the Index </A>`

- If you use **TARGET** = **_top** or **TARGET** = **_parent**, the incoming document will replace a layout document. This will also need a return link:

  `<A HREF = topframe.htm> Return to the Home Page </A>`

The page in the next screenshot uses this Index document. (I've pruned some of the links to save space and because they don't show anything new.)

```
<HTML>
<HEAD><H2> Index </H2></HEAD>
<BODY>
<UL>
<B>Ingrid's stuff</B>
<LI><A HREF = ingrid.htm TARGET = contents>
Ingrid's Home Page</A>
<LI><A HREF = views.htm TARGET = _blank>
Dribble Views </A>
<LI><A HREF = ggnome.htm TARGET = contents>
The Green Gnome </A>
<P>
<B>Demos</B>
<LI><A HREF = emphasis.htm TARGET = contents> Empha-
sizing Text </A>
<LI><A HREF = lines.htm TARGET = contents> Horizontal
Rules </A>
<LI><A HREF = list.htm TARGET = contents> Simple List </A>
<LI><A HREF = deflist.htm TARGET = contents> Definition
List </A>
<LI><A HREF = clee.htm TARGET = contents> Graphics and
Links </A>
<LI><A HREF = table4.htm TARGET = contents> Table with
Headings </A>
<P> <B> Other </B>
<LI><A HREF = machome.htm TARGET = _top>
Mac's Home Page</A>
</UL>
</BODY>
</HTML>
```

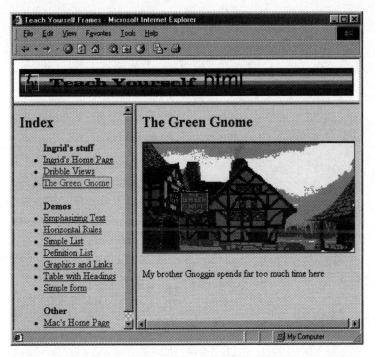

At this point, one of the Ingrid links has been clicked, displaying the page in the contents frame.

Contents pages

Any of your existing HTML documents can be displayed in the *contents* frame, or wherever you choose to target them. If you have designed them to work in windows of any size, then the fact that they are displayed in a frame, not the full screen, should not matter.

As noted already, you may need to do a little editing:

● Where a page replaces the inner or the top layout document, you must link back to it to restore the original frame structure.

● If you want the site to be viewable in older browsers, you must provide links between the pages, so that visitors can still navigate between them.

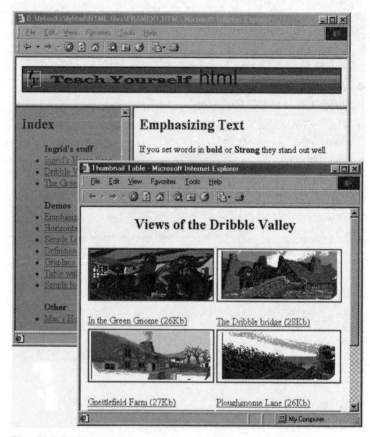

The TARGET = _blank option for the Green Gnome link has opened a new browser window to display it.

- If you are including links to other people's pages, these will not have links back to you (unless you have arranged it with them). These must be targeted into your contents area or a new blank window, so that your index frame remains visible, if you want your visitors to be able to get back to you.

Summary

◆ Frame displays are much easier to set up than you might think at first sight.

◆ With frames, the structure is created in layout documents; the display in contents documents.

◆ The <FRAMESET> tag defines the number and size of the divisions.

◆ The <FRAME> tag specifies the (layout or contents) document to use when the frame is first opened.

◆ Frames should be given NAMEs, if they are to be the TARGET for an incoming page.

◆ In a frame display, you normally use one frame to hold an index, for your visitors to navigate through your pages.

Image maps and frames

There is another example of frames – this time using an image map as an index – at the end of the next chapter.

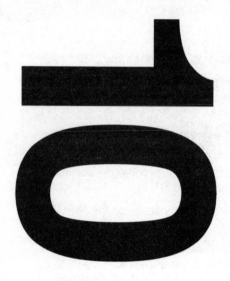

10

image maps

In this unit you will learn

- how image maps work
- how to create image maps
- how to use image maps in framed pages

10.1 Drawing the map

A good image map can give a slick professional appearance to your home page – and a bad one can really put visitors off! The difference is all in the design, and I can't help much there. What I can do is look at the practical aspects of producing an image map. There are two ways of going about it. The easy way is to get a bit of software to do the job for you; the hard way is to do it all yourself – though even that is not so hard.

There aren't any rules on what sort of image you can use as a map. The graphic can be a photograph, scanned image or painted picture; it can be an integrated design or a collection of small images on a common background; plain or fancy text can be added if desired. All that is essential is that you keep its purpose in mind, and work towards that. Your visitors should be able to identify easily where they should click and what will happen when they click there.

The Status line shows us that the top left of the Green Gnome picture is at 188, 176. Record these co-ordinates if you are taking the DIY route.

If you have MapEdit (see page 156), or other image map software, all you need to do after creating the image is convert it into a GIF file. If you are doing it all yourself, go over the image and note the co-ordinates of the top left and bottom right corners of the areas that hold each clickable part.

10.2 The map page

An image map can sit at the top of a much longer home page, or it can fit into a frame, or it can form a home page by itself. However you do it, your page should also include plain text links to the same places, so that visitors can still get there, even if they choose not to load the image.

In the example page here, I have used the same background colour – black – for the page, as for the image. This helps to give a uniform appearance to the page, though once the image map has been set up properly, it will be distinguished from the background by an outline in the text colour. Note that the LINK and VLINK colours have had to be changed so that the links are visible.

The other minor point worth noting here is the way that the links have been separated. I have put * – any character would have done – between each pair so that they do not form a continuous line of text.

```
<HTML>
<HEAD>
<TITLE> Image Map </TITLE>
</HEAD>
<BODY BGCOLOR="000000" TEXT="FFFFFF"
LINK="FFFF00" VLINK="00FFFF">
<P ALIGN = CENTER>
<IMG SRC="imagemap.gif">      These 4 pages will be
</P>                           linked from the image map
<A HREF="machome.htm">Mac </A> *
<A HREF="tylogo.htm">Teach Yourself </A> *
<A HREF="ingrid.htm">Ingrid's Home Page </A> *
<A HREF="soton.htm"> What's on in Soton </A>
```

```
    </BODY>
    </HTML>
```

Save the file at this stage and check its appearance in your browser. When you are happy with the design, move on.

The basic HTML document, with its image, before mapping.

10.3 Linking code

The first job is to define which graphic is to be the image map. The graphic needs a name by which it will be known inside the document. It may as well be based on the filename, but could be anything – though it must be a single word and start with #.

Inside the <IMG SRC ...> tag, you add the option USEMAP = giving the image map's name.

```
    <IMG SRC = mymap.gif  USEMAP = #mymap>
```

This name is picked up again at the start of the mapping section. This is marked by the <MAP NAME = ...> tag.

```
    <MAP NAME = mymap>
```

Note that the # is omitted here. The use of # in map names reflects its use in the names of jump points (see Chapter 4).

Inside the <MAP ...> section, you define each area of the map which is to carry a link. The definitions look like this:

```
<AREA SHAPE = "rect" COORDS = "15,120,115,240" HREF
= "machome.htm">
```

Let's break that line down into its parts:

<AREA   marks the start of the tag;

SHAPE =   either *rect*, *circle*, *polygon* or *default*

COORDS =   are the co-ordinates that define the shape.

HREF = ...> the URL of the page to be linked to the area.

Co-ordinates

The pattern of co-ordinates depends upon the shape. Working from the shapes in the diagram below:

for *rect*, give the top left and bottom right corners; e.g.

    COORDS = 25, 25, 100, 75

for *circle* give the centre, followed by the radius; e.g.

    COORDS = 200, 50, 25

for *polygon*, give the x,y co-ordinates of each point: e.g.

    COORDS = 100, 100, 200, 100, 150, 50, 100, 100

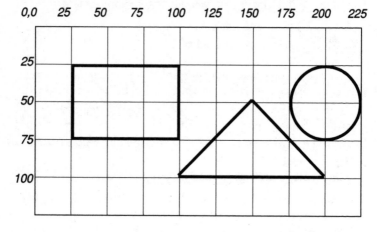

The background of the image – everything not enclosed by a shape – can be refered to as *default*. You can also link a page to here, or if you do not want this to be 'clickable', set it to NOHREF.

<AREA SHAPE = "default" NOHREF>

If you haven't yet worked out the co-ordinates of the clickable areas on your map, load the image back into your graphics application and read the co-ordinates off the Status line as you point to the corners of the areas.

Mark the end of the <MAP ...> section with the tag </MAP>.

The example given here works for my image map only.

```
<HTML>
<HEAD>
<TITLE> Image Map </TITLE>
</HEAD>
<BODY BGCOLOR="000000" TEXT="FFFFFF"
LINK="FFFF00" VLINK="00FFFF">
<P ALIGN = CENTER>
<IMG SRC = "imagemap.gif" USEMAP = "#imagemap"> <P>
<A HREF = "machome.htm">Mac </A> *
<A HREF = "tylogo.htm">Teach Yourself </A> *
<A HREF = "ingrid.htm">Ingrid's Home Page </A> *
<A HREF = "soton.htm"> What's on in Soton </A>
<MAP NAME = "imagemap">
<AREA SHAPE = "rect" COORDS = "15,120,115,240" HREF
= "machome.htm">
<AREA SHAPE = "rect" COORDS = "210,20,280,90" HREF
= "tylogo.htm">
<AREA SHAPE = "rect" COORDS = "190,170,330,250"
HREF = "ingrid.htm">
<AREA SHAPE = "circle" COORDS = "175,160,25" HREF =
"soton.htm">
<AREA SHAPE = "default" NOHREF>
</MAP>
</BODY>
</HTML>
```

10.4 MapEdit

If that last section has left you feeling that there ought to be an easier way to set up image maps, then this section is for you. MapEdit, from Boutell Inc., is a simple, effective and cheap ($25 in 2002) solution. Get an evaluation copy from them at:

http://www.boutell.com/mapedit

MapEdit is available for Windows, Apple Mac, Linux and Unix systems. Select the one you need and download it from their home page. It comes in as a small self-extracting ZIP file – the latest Windows version is just under 280Kb.

To use MapEdit, first prepare your map image and place it in an HTML document – any required text or text links can also be added at this stage. Save the document and run MapEdit.

Give the **File > Open** command, and at the **Open** dialog box, browse for the HTML file containing your map.

MapEdit will scan the file and pick up any image references. You will then be asked which one to map. (The document could have any number of images in it – for that matter, you could set up several maps on different images in one document.)

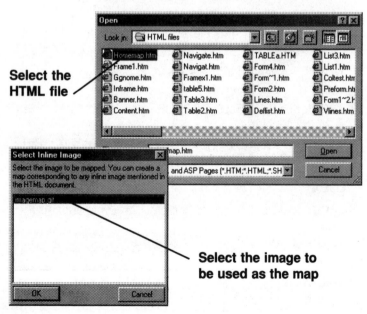

Select the HTML file

Select the image to be used as the map

Once the image is loaded in, you can start to create clickable areas on it. Select a shape tool, then click the top left corner and drag and click on the bottom right corners for a rectangle, click the centre and drag and click to the edge for a circle, or click the sequence of points for a polygon.

After the last click, MapEdit asks for details of the URL to be linked to that area. ALT text, for visitors who don't load graphics, can be defined at this stage, and if you are working in frames, you can also set the TARGET for the linked page to be displayed in.

As you add areas, their outlines remain visible – these will not be displayed in the working map. Shapes can overlap, but note that a click in the overlap area will select the first area to have been defined.

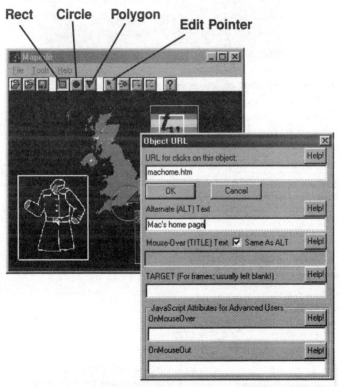

If afterwards you need to change a shape, or its URL, use the Edit Pointer to select the area then make your alterations.

When you have finished, save the file. If you then open it in your word-processor, you will see that MapEdit has written the code for you. If necessary, you can make further adjustments or addition 'by hand'.

10.5 Image maps in frames

This next example is mainly to show how image maps can be used to navigate within frames, but it is also a good opportunity to revisit the frame concept.

The aim is to produce a screen that carries a logo, a title bar and an image map, in three frames around a main display area. We start with a sketch, to work out the structure of frames.

The logo area is approximately 200 × 200 pixels. The titlebar can be flexible in size, but should occupy about 15% of the height. That leads us to these layout documents:

outframe.htm

```
<HTML>
<TITLE>cOn-Line </TITLE>
<FRAMESET COLS = 200,*>
 <FRAME SRC = left.htm NORESIZE SCROLLING = Yes>
 <FRAME SRC = right.htm SCROLLING = Auto>
</FRAMESET>
</HTML>
```

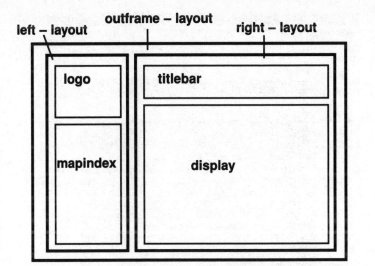

left – layout

outframe – layout

right – layout

logo

titlebar

mapindex

display

The planning sketch for the image map/framed page.

left.htm

width of logo frame

```
<HTML>
<FRAMESET ROWS = 200,*>
 <FRAME SRC = logo.htm NORESIZE SCROLLING = No>
 <FRAME SRC = mapindex.htm SCROLLING = Auto>
</FRAMESET>
</HTML>
```

right.htm

height of logo frame

```
<HTML>
<FRAMESET ROWS = 15%,*>
 <FRAME SRC = titlebar.htm NORESIZE SCROLLING =
No>
 <FRAME SRC = display.htm NAME = display>
</FRAMESET>
</HTML>
```

The contents of the logo, titlebar and display documents are irrelevant – you can see what I have used in the illustration on the next page. My example firm, cOn-line, is one of those who aim to make money from the gullible. You can probably guess that from the image map.

The image map/framed page seen in a browser. It's not actually a very well-balanced page when you look at in a normal – i.e. wider than high – browser window.

The index image map, seen here in MapEdit, links to three documents that will be targeted at the display window.

Note that the target is set in the TARGET slot of the **Object URL** dialog box.

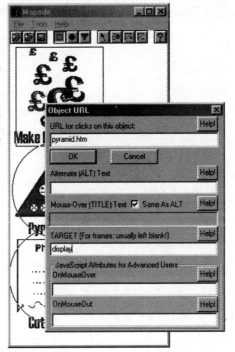

There is another image map in this page – the logo in the top left has been mapped so that if it is clicked, the welcome document is reloaded into the *display* frame. It is useful to have a means of restoring a display if visitors can wander off down routes that do not lead directly back. If incoming documents overwrite the *right* layout document, then the restore link should be targeted to that whole area.

```
<HTML>
<IMG SRC = "conlogo.gif" USEMAP = "#conlogo">
<MAP NAME = "conlogo">
<AREA SHAPE = "rect" COORDS = "1,1,150,150" HREF =
"display.htm" TARGET = display>
<AREA SHAPE = "default" NOHREF>
</MAP>
</HTML>
```

Summary

◆ Any graphic can be used as an image map, though it must be in GIF or JPG format, and should be easily understood by your visitors.

◆ An image map can sit anywhere in a page. You can have several image maps in the same document, if required.

◆ You should provide text link alternatives to the map, for those visitors that cannot or do not want to download graphics.

◆ Image maps are defined with the <MAP NAME = ...> tag.

◆ Each clickable area must be set up with an <AREA...> tag, giving the co-ordinates to define its outline.

◆ The MapEdit program, from Boutell Inc., offers an easy way to create image maps.

◆ Image maps can be a good way to navigate through a frame display.

11

style sheets

In this unit you will learn

- how framed pages work
- how to create simple and nested framed pages
- how to display linked pages

11.1 What are style sheets?

Style sheets were introduced with HTML 4.0, and give us far more control over our displays. They can be used for the normal text and paragraph formatting, but also for controlling:

● text size and spacing – between letters, words and lines;

● margins, borders and background colours for the page and for paragraphs;

● the way images appear in the background of a page, and the use of images as bullets for lists.

There are a number of style sheet languages, each extending HTML in its own special way. The most important of these is CSS1 – Cascading Style Sheets, version 1. Its standards have been implemented in Internet Explorer and Netscape Navigator, from version 4.0 onwards, and that's the only one we need to know about.

Style sheets work by allowing you to redefine tags. For example, you could redefine <H1> so that text enclosed in this tag was displayed in Arial, coloured red and centre aligned instead of Times, black and on the left.

It is a 'cascading' system because you can have any number of style sheets in a page – a 'style sheet' is simply a definition of one or more styles – and formatting is passed on from one sheet to the next.

The <P> tag, for instance, might have styles applied to it at three points in a document. The first style sheet might set the colour, font size and margins; the second set the margins; the third set the colour and background colour. The final display will take the font size from the first, margins from the second and its colours from the third style sheet.

With multiple style sheets and restyling you can set different formats within a document. In large organizations, you can have one style sheet to set the basic common format for the whole site, a second to set the variations for a department, a third to set a special format to suit an individual document, and further restyling within it to pick out particular items.

Specifying style sheets

There are three ways that you can set up a STYLE:

● write the style specifications in a STYLE block – the main way that we will be using;

● use the STYLE keyword within a tag to redefine it, e.g.

    `<P STYLE="color: blue">This paragraph is blue.</P>`

● link to or import an external style sheet (see page 182).

STYLE blocks

A STYLE block consists of the **<STYLE>...</STYLE>** pair enclosing a set of styling lines. The block can be written anywhere in the document, but is normally placed in the **HEAD** area. It can be written in the BODY area, but must be <!commented out> to stop it being displayed by older browsers.

Here's a simple **STYLE** block:

```
<STYLE TYPE=text/css>
        H1 { text-align:center; color: red }
</STYLE>
```

TYPE = **text/css** specifies the language – *Cascading Style Sheets.*

A style definition starts with a tag name – without <brackets> – followed by one or more styles given as '*attribute:format*', separated by semi-colons and enclosed in {curly brackets}. The *attribute* defines which aspect of the style to set, and the *format* says how it should look. Spaces can be used freely within the defintion to improve readability – they are ignored by the browser. The example line redefines <H1> so that it is centred and coloured red, but it will be in the default font and size as these have not been redefined.

There are around 50 attributes and nearly 100 format options, but they are not things that you will normally use very often – look them up in the Summary when you need them!

Elements and inheritance

In style sheet jargon, an *element* is a tag and the text or image affected by it. The BODY itself, an <H...> heading, a <P>

paragraph, a <B>bold</B> item within a block of text – all are elements.

An element within another, such as bold text within a paragraph, is the *child* of the containing element – which is its *parent*. And children inherit characteristics from their parents. So, if the <P> tag has been defined as blue, 14 point, the <B> bold text is also blue and 14 point – unless these formats have been redefined by styling the <B> tag.

The following code shows inheritance at work. We'll get back to the details of formatting shortly, so don't worry about that, but focus on how styles are inherited and overriden.

● The **BODY** style sets yellow text on a red background.

● **P** sets the background to blue and centre-aligns the text.

● **H1** redefines the font name but takes the text colour from the **BODY** setting.

● **B** sets the text to white and uppercase but retains its parent background colour – red within untagged text and blue within the P element.

```
<HTML>
<HEAD>
<TITLE>Inheritance</TITLE>
<STYLE type=text/css>
    BODY {background-color:red; color:yellow}
    P {background-color:blue;text-align:center}
    H1 {font-family: arial, sans-serif}
    B {color:white; text-transform:uppercase}
</STYLE>
</HEAD>
<BODY>
<H1>Inheritance</H1>
```

color – US spelling

Untagged text takes the <B>body</B> style - yellow on a red background, and left-aligned by default.

<P>Inside a P tag, the P style settings override those set at BODY level, the background is now blue and the text centre-aligned.</P>

<P>An element inside another is its child <B> and may have a child of its own. </B> B inherits the blue background from P but has changed the text to red and upper case.</P>
</BODY>
</HTML>

\<B> white, capitals

\<P> blue background, centred

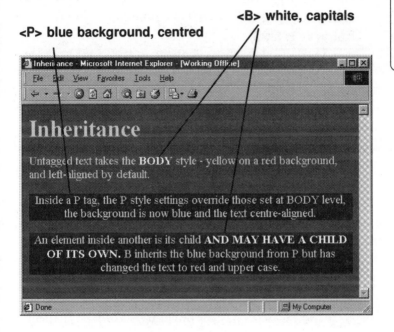

11.2 Font attributes

With style sheets you can specify the typeface, style, weight and size of your text.

font-family

A <FONT FACE = > tag will fail if the font is not present on the browser that is viewing the page. The *font-family* attribute gets round this by allowing you to give a list of alternatives, which should end with a generic name. When the page is viewed, the browser will work through the list and use the first named that it can, or otherwise use one of the generic type.

Font names should be written as they appear in your system, enclosed in "double quotes" if there are spaces in the name.

The generic names are:

serif (e.g. Times New Roman),

sans-serif (e.g. Arial),

cursive (e.g. *Lucida Calligraphy*),

fantasy (e.g. Playbill)

monospace (e.g. Courier New).

This line sets the <P> text to a sans serif font, preferably Arial or Helvetica.

    P {font-family: arial, helvetica, sans-serif}

Other attributes

font-style can be *italic*, *normal* or *oblique*.

font-weight gives you levels of 'boldness'. It can be set by:

the keywords *lighter, normal, bold* or *bolder*,

or by the numbers 100, 200, 300 … to 900, with 500 being normal and 900 the heaviest type.

font-size can be set by:

the keywords *xx-small, x-small, small, medium, large, x-large* or *xx-large* (equivalent to HTML sizes 1 to 7),

or *larger* or *smaller* (which set the size relative to the parent element),

or by a percentage based on the line-height (see page 170).

e.g. to make the H2 headings italic, a fairly heavy bold, size 5:

    H2 {font-style:italic; font-weight:700; font-size:large}

When working with the next example, try different size, weight and font family settings to see the effects. Also, try defining different attributes within the <B STYLE = …> tag. You should see that those that could have an impact outside the tag – e.g. weight and size – cannot be redefined.

    <HTML>
    <HEAD>

```
<TITLE>Formatting Fonts</TITLE>
<STYLE type=text/css>
    BODY {font-family: "Lucida Sans", Helvetica, sans-serif}
    H1 {font-family: "Lucida Calligraphy", cursive; font-size:x-
large}
    H2 {font-style:italic; font-size:16pt}
    P {font-family:Georgia, "Times New Roman",serif; font-
size:14pt; font-weight:400}
    B {font-weight:bolder}
</STYLE>
</HEAD>


<BODY>
<H1>Formatting Fonts</H1>
<H2>Set the face, size, and <B>style</B></H2>
Remember that if you don't use P tags, <B>text takes the
BODY style</B>.
<P>And that within any tags you can restyle an element <B
STYLE = color:red> - even within the tag itself</B>
</BODY>
</HTML>
```

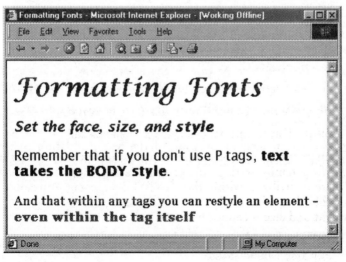

Text attributes

These relate to the layout of text and can be applied alongside any font styles.

text-align is identical to the HTML **ALIGN** option, taking the keyword *left*, *right*, *center* and *justify*.

text-indent sets the indent of the first line of a paragraph. The length can be given in em (width of the letter 'm'), cm, px (pixels) or as a percentage of the element's width.

line-height sets the distance between the baselines of text. It can be given as:

- the keyword *normal*, setting it to 120% of the font height;
- a *number*, which is multiplied by the font size; e.g. for 1½ line-spacing:

    ```
    P {line-height:1.5}
    ```

- a *percentage*, again multiplied by the font size; e.g. for double-spacing:

    ```
    P {line-height:200%}
    ```

- a *fixed size*, in units of em, cm or px.

When the line height is given as a number, the line height in any child elements are multiplied by the same number; in other cases, the resultant height is inherited.

text-decoration has three settings – *underline* and *line-through* and *overline*.

text-transform sets the case of characters, using the keywords *capitalize* (capital first letter only), *uppercase*, *lowercase* or *none*.

word-spacing sets the distance between words; **letter-spacing** sets the distance between letters in a word. Both are set in ems.

vertical-align sets the position of the text in relation to the baseline. There are several keywords of which only *sub* (subscript) and *super* (superscript) have any noticeable effect.

```
<HTML>
<HEAD>
<TITLE>Text attributes</TITLE>
<STYLE type=text/css>
```

```
BODY {text-align:center}

H1 {text-transform:capitalize; text-decoration:underline}

P {text-align:left; text-indent:2cm;font-size:12pt; line-
height:180%}

</STYLE>

</HEAD>

<BODY>

<BR>

<H1>The headline should be underlined with initial capitals

</H1>

Everything in the body is centre-aligned.

<P>Unless it has been given a different alignment - text in
the P tag will be left-aligned. It is also indented 2cm, and in
12pt.</P>

</BODY>

</HTML>
```

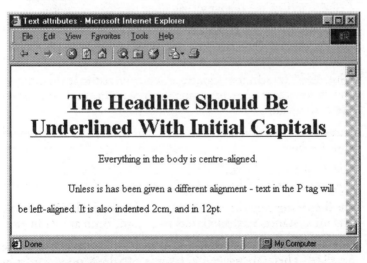

11.3 Backgrounds and borders

color sets the colour of text, lines and borders. Colours can be
given as one of the standard names (page 38), or by using the
expression **rgb(*red_val, green_val, blue_val*)**. The values are
in the range 0 to 255 – normal numbers, not hexadecimal.

```
BODY {color:white}
P {color:rgb(192,0,192)}
```

These set white as the default colour for text and borders, and lilac (lots of red and blue, but no green) for the paragraph text.

Backgrounds

You can set background colours and images for any tag, as well as for the page. The attributes are always set in the same way.

background-color takes a colour name, an **rgb(*val,val,val*)** expression or the keyword *transparent*.

background-image takes the expression **URL(*image_url*)** and *image_url* can be the name or a local file or one on the Web.

background-repeat defines how the image is shown. *repeat* sets full screen tiling; *repeat-x* duplicates it across the top; *repeat-y* produces a strip down the left; *no-repeat* sets a single image.

```
BODY {background-image: URL(logo.gif); background-
repeat:repeat; background-color:silver}
```

This tiles the screen with the logo image, or colours the background pale grey if images are not loaded by the browser.

background-attachment can be set to *scroll*, so that the image moves with the text, or *fixed*, so that it stays in place when the page is scrolled.

background-position set the horizontal and vertical placing, either by the keywords *top*, *center*, *bottom*, *left*, *center* or *right*, or by giving the length in cm or px from the top left corner.

```
<HTML>
<HEAD>
<TITLE>Backgrounds</TITLE>
<STYLE type=text/css>
  BODY {background-image:URL(stars.gif); background-
repeat:repeat}
  H1 {background-image:URL(stripes.gif); color:black; text-
align:center}
  P {color:white;font-size:large}
  B {background-color:red; color:white}
</STYLE>
```

```
</HEAD>
<BODY>
<BR>
<H1>! Stars and Stripes !</H1>
<P>And other decorative backgrounds can be applied to the
whole page, and/or <B>tagged text.</B>
</BODY>
</HTML>
```

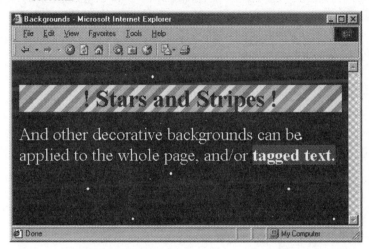

Margins and borders

All *block elements* – the BODY, images, tables, headings, <P>
and other tags that create paragraphs – have margins, borders
and padding.

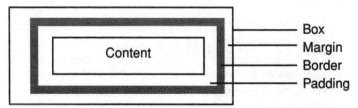

For the BODY element, the box is the edge of the page; for
other elements, the box is the padding of the parent element,
unless you set its size. You can also use the attributes **width**

and **height** for this. Values are given in the usual em, cm or px units, or as a percentage of the limits of the parent element.

The margin, border and padding all have *width,* which can be anything from 0 upwards. If there is no border, the combined margin and padding values determine the amount of space around the content.

The simplest approach is to set all four sides the same, e.g.

```
P {margin:10%; border-width:5px; padding:0.2cm}
```

This gives <P> text a margin all round of 10%, a border of 5 pixels, and padding of 0.2cm.

The widths of the four sides can be set separately, giving them in the order: top, right, bottom, left. If only two or three are given, the missing values are taken from the opposite sides.

```
P {margin: 5% 10%; padding:0.2cm 0.5cm 0.1cm; border-
width 20}
```

This sets the margins to the top and bottom at 5%, to the left and right margins at 10%; padding of 0.2cm at the top, 0.5cm to left and right and 0.1cm at the bottom; and a border of 20 pixels all round.

Border colour and style

border-color sets the colour of the whole border. Sides can be coloured individually by specifying **border-top-color**, **border-left-color**, **border-right-color** and **border-bottom-color**.

border-style can be set to **solid**, **double**, **groove**, **ridge**, **inset**, **outset** or **none**. Note that you need widths of 6 pixels or more to see most of these effects.

Internet Explorer and margins

For reasons best known to itself, Internet Explorer does not handle the **margin** options properly. On the **body** element, it adds the margins *inside* the border, and for other elements, it only applies the margins to the sides.

```
<HTML>
<HEAD>
<TITLE>Margins and borders</TITLE>
<STYLE type=text/css>
    BODY {border-color:lime; border-width:0.5cm; border-
        style:ridge; padding:0.25 cm; text-align:center}
    H1 {border-color:red;border-width:8 16 8 16; border-
        style:inset; color:blue; padding:0.5cm}
    P {margin:.5cm;width:80%;border-width:6px; border-
        style:double; padding:0.5cm}
</STYLE>
</HEAD>
<BODY>
<H1>Margins and borders</H1>
<P>Borders can add colour to a page, or pick out an item for
special attention.
</BODY>
</HTML>
```

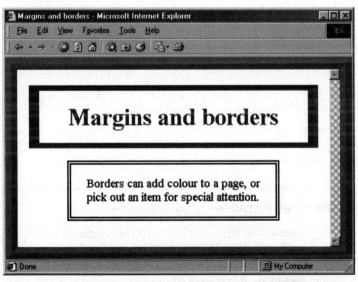

This looks much better in colour! Experiment with different style settings and colours to see how they affect the appearance.

11.4 Classes and IDs

Classes and IDs bring infinite variety to pages, as they let you apply any number of styles to the same HTML tag. For example, write these definitions in the **STYLE** block:

```
H1 {font-size:30pt; color:green}

H1.redhead {font-style:italic; color:red}

H1.bluehead {color:blue}
```

and you will then have three <**H1**> tag styles. Within the **BODY** they are used like this:

```
<H1>This heading is 30 point in green</H1>

<H1 CLASS = redhead>This is 30 point in red italics</H1>

<H1 CLASS = bluehead>This is 30 point in blue</H1>
```

All classes of <**H1**> inherit the default settings for the tag and any styles applied to the basic tag, but settings defined for a class override any inherited ones.

ID

Here is another way to create a format that can be applied to any tag. Define it in the **STYLE** area – note # before the name:

```
#redbox {border-color:red; border-width:10px; padding:5px}
```

Apply as required, using the **ID** keyword and the name, without the #:

```
<H2 ID = redbox>This is important</H2>


<HTML>

<HEAD>

<TITLE>Class and ID</TITLE>

<STYLE type=text/css>

    H2.bluehead {font-weight:800;color:blue}

    P {font-size:14pt; font-style:italic}

    P.parared {color:red; font-style:normal}

    p.paraheavy{font-weight:800}

    #boxed {border-width:6; border-style:solid; padding: 5;
border-color:red}
```

```
</STYLE>
</HEAD>
<BODY>
<H2>Class and ID</H2>
<P>Classes allow you to have a greater range of styles
<H2 CLASS= bluehead>Same tag, different effect</H2>
<P CLASS = parared>Classes inherit styles from simple tag
definitions
<H2 ID = boxed>IDs extend</H2>
<P ID = boxed>With an ID you can apply the same format-
ting to different tags
<P CLASS = paraheavy ID = boxed> and you can use both
at once
</BODY>
</HTML>
```

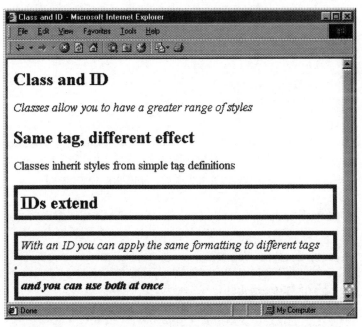

Setting colours is a very visible way to test the effect of class
definitions – but only on screen!

11.5 <DIV> and <SPAN>

These tags were introduced along with style sheets. They can be used to format sections of code.

<DIV> </DIV>

<DIV> marks off a division of the page in which a special format can be applied. It can be used as a simple HTML tag:

```
<DIV ALIGN = center>
    ... text and images all centred in here ...
</DIV>
```

More usefully, <DIV> can take STYLE specifications. This sets up a section in which the text is right-aligned and coloured red (unless other tags are applied to elements within it).

```
<DIV STYLE = text-align:right;color:red>
```

DIV can also be formatted through a class or ID definition in the STYLE block.

```
DIV.cent {text-align:centre; font-size:16pt; font-style:italic}
...
<DIV CLASS = cent>
    text will be centred, italic in 16 point
</DIV>
```

The same effect could be achieved by using an ID – and the ID style could also be applied to any other suitable tag.

```
#cent {text-align:centre; font-size:16pt; font-style:italic}
...
<DIV ID = cent>
    ...
<P ID = cent>
```

<SPAN> </SPAN>

<SPAN> marks off sections *within* blocks of text, e.g.

```
Stop when the lights are <SPAN STYLE = color:red>red
</SPAN> and wait for them to change.
```

SPAN can be also defined through a class or ID.

```
SPAN.loud {font-size:18pt; font-weight:800}

    ...

        This is really <SPAN CLASS = loud>important</SPAN>
```

The next example demonstrates <DIV> and <SPAN>.

```
<HTML>
<HEAD>
<TITLE>Div and Span</TITLE>
 <STYLE type=text/css>
  P {font-size:18pt; font-face:arial}
  SPAN.initial {font-size:30pt; font-face:serif; color:black }
  DIV.standout{color:green; font-style:italic; border-width:10;
    border-style:ridge}
 </STYLE>
</HEAD>
<BODY>
<H1>The Spider's Web</H1>
<DIV STYLE = color:red>
  <P><SPAN class=initial>O</SPAN>nce upon a time there
was a <SPAN STYLE = font-size:10pt>very small</SPAN>
Web ...</P>
</DIV>
This tale of how a little spider called Hotmetal span a web
and span it some more until it covered the whole world, is
available now from all good bookstores
<P>
<DIV CLASS=standout ALIGN = center>
  or direct from <SPAN class=initial>C</SPAN>ern <SPAN
class=initial> S</SPAN>tory <SPAN class=initial>S</
SPAN>tore
</DIV>
</BODY>
</HTML>
```

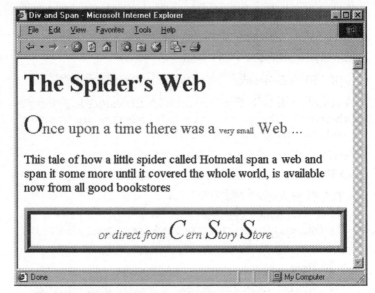

One of the most obvious uses of SPAN in this example is in the initial class that creates the large initial letters.

11.6 Layers

The basic idea behind layers is simple – by adding position information to a tag, you locate an element anywhere on screen. The elements are displayed in the order that they appear in the code, with later ones overlapping earlier – in layers. In theory, you can set a position on any tag, but in practice, it only really works with <DIV> and <SPAN>. This is not a big problem – if you wanted to locate a multi-line block of text, you'd have to use <DIV>, and it just means two extra lines round images.

The hard work is getting things in the right place! Planning the layout helps, but trial and error gets you there in the end. (And don't forget that if the page is going onto the Web, people will be viewing it in a wide range of window sizes.)

position can be set **absolute** – measured from the top left of the window or of its containing element (**DIV**s can be nested) – or **relative** – measured from the bottom left corner of the previous layer. The **top** and **left** distances can be given in em, cm or px units.

You can define the layer as a class in the **STYLE** area:

    DIV.flow {position:absolute; top:200px; left:300px}

or directly within the **<DIV>** tag

    <DIV STYLE=position:absolute; top:100px; left:100px>

An example will help. Experiment with the values and order to see the effect. Change the order in which they are written in the code to change the layering order.

```
<HTML>
<HEAD>
<TITLE>Layers</TITLE>
<STYLE type=text/css>
    H1 {text-align:center; border-width:6px; border-
style:ridge; border-color:blue; background-color:lime}
    B {font-weight:800; font-size:14pt; color:red}
    P {border-width:5px; border-style:solid; padding:10px;
border-color:red; background-color:yellow}
    DIV.pic {position:absolute; top:20px; left:50px}
    DIV.eggtext {position:absolute; top:275px; left:225px}
</STYLE>
</HEAD>
<BODY>
<H1>Layers</H1>
<DIV CLASS = pic> <IMG SRC = chicken.gif> </DIV>
<DIV STYLE="position:absolute; top:150px; left:100px">
    <P>Which came first? The chicken...
</DIV>
<DIV STYLE="position:absolute; top:180px; left:300px">
    <IMG SRC = egg.gif>
</DIV>
<DIV CLASS = eggtext>
    <P> ... or the egg</P>
</DIV>
</BODY>
</HTML>
```

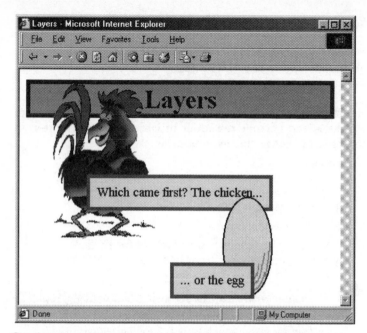

Overlapping makes the use of layers very visible, but the real point is that you can place elements exactly where you want them. Notice that positions can be defined in the STYLE block or in the DIV tag – use whichever gives more readable code.

11.7 External style sheets

One big advantage of style sheets is that they make it much simpler to create and maintain consistency across a site. The site's designer can set up free-standing style sheets, containing nothing but definitions, which can be linked into pages to set styles. The linking lines look like this:

```
<LINK REL=STYLESHEET TYPE=text/css HREF=corp.css>
```

There might just be one sheet for the whole site, or one sheet to set the overall corporate design, then a number of second level ones for departments – and perhaps third or fourth level ones too. The lower level sheets will normally be there to adjust the basic design, not replace it. The design can be tweaked further by **STYLE** settings within the pages.

The **<LINK>** and **<STYLE>** tags must be written in cascading order. Settings are applied as the code is processed, so that later settings override earlier ones. In the next example, the overall sheet is linked first. Its settings are modified by the sales department's sheet, which is linked next. Final adjustments to the formats are then made through STYLE setting.

Creating a style sheet file

Definitions of tags, classes and IDs are written in exactly the same way as in a **STYLE** area, though without the **<STYLE>** tags. A style sheet file could hold a comprehensive redefinition of a whole range of tags, along with the creation of classes for every occasion, or it might just define one or two aspects. The main advantage of a style sheet file is that it can be used to control the appearance of many pages, and redefining that one file will reformat every page that is linked to it.

Comments to identify the sheet or explain formats can be added as required, but should be written inside **/*** … ***/** markers. The file is saved as text, with a **.css** extension.

Here's the first sheet, which sets the corporate styles.

```
/* corporate style sheet  */
    BODY {background-color:yellow}
    P {font-size:14pt; margin-left:10px; margin-right:20px}
    H1, H2, H3, H4 {font-family:tahoma,arial,sans-serif; text-align:center}
    ADDRESS {background-color:red;padding:5px; border-width:5px; border-style:groove; border-color:blue}
```

The next sheet gives the department's variations, which simply change some colours, leaving all the size and layout formatting untouched.

```
/* departmental style sheet for Sales */
    P {color:maroon}
    H1, H2, H3, H4 {color:navy}
    ADDRESS {border-color:navy}
```

And now for the code itself. This links in the two style sheets, then redefines some features of some text tags.

```
<HTML>
<HEAD>
  <TITLE>External style sheets</TITLE>
<!The two external sheets are linked>

  <LINK REL=STYLESHEET TYPE=text/css HREF=corp.css>
  <LINK REL=STYLESHEET TYPE=text/css HREF=sales.css>
<!Then the special styles for the page are defined>
  <STYLE TYPE = text/css>

    H1, H2 {border-width:4; border-style:solid; background-
color:white}

    P {font-weight:bold; background-color:lime}

    ADDRESS {text-align:center}

    </STYLE>
</HEAD>


  <BODY>
    <H1>Colossal Summer Savings!</H1>

    <H2>Special Offers</H2>

    <H3>Domain Names</H3>

    <P>Buy One Get One Free! Choose from .TV, .CO, .IT
and .IN

    <H3>Web site design</H3>

    <P>From concept to completion, full service, satisfaction
guaranteed. <BR>

    Start July or August to get a 20% discount and be ready
for Xmas</P>

<ADDRESS>E-mail your order to <A HREF = mailto:
sales@webs.con>WebSpinners</A> now </ADDRESS>

  </BODY>
</HTML>
```

Compare the resulting display with the two style sheet files
and the HTML code to see which features are set at which
stage. What would be the effect of linking the sheet files in a
different order?

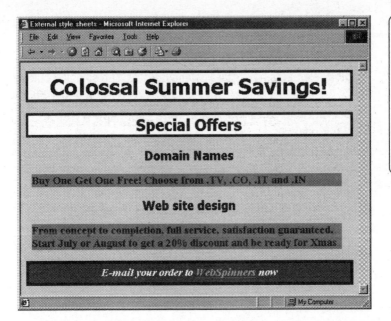

Create one or more other pages, also linking in the two style sheet files, but with different local STYLE definitions. Then change the definitions in the style sheet files and you see how easy it could be to give your site a face lift!

Summary

◆ Style sheets allow you to redefine tags, giving fuller control over the appearance and positioning of text and images.

◆ An element is a tagged section of code. Paragraphs, heading and images are block elements; items within paragraphs are inline elements.

◆ When an element is enclosed by another, they have a parent–child relationship in which style definitions in the parent element are inherited by the child.

◆ The font attributes have the same formatting options as <FONT> and other HTML styling tags, plus greater control over weight and size.

◆ The text attributes set the alignment and spacing of text.

◆ Style sheets let you set a background colour for a paragraph, different from that of the body. Where an image is used as a body background, its repetition and position can be controlled.

◆ Block elements have margins and borders. The size and colour of these can be set to enable the accurate placing of elements.

◆ Classes and IDs allow you to have alternative styles for the same element.

◆ A style can be defined so that it only applies to an element when it is within another element, for example, how bold is displayed within a particular heading.

◆ The <DIV> and <SPAN> tags allow you to set styles within a restricted area of the page. <DIV> can also be used to position elements in (overlapping) layers in the page.

◆ Where consistent styles are required in sets of pages, external style sheets can be linked in.

12

active pages

In this unit you will learn

- how to create and use animated GIFs
- how JavaScript code can be used on Web pages
- how Java applets can be embedded in pages

12.1 Animated GIFs

These are perhaps the easiest way to liven up a static page. An animated GIF is a set of GIF images, which are stored as one file, and displayed in succession at timed intervals. Any modern browser can display them, and any decent graphics software can be used to create the set of images, but you do need special software to turn them into an animation.

The images

These should be all the same size and saved in the standard GIF format. How many you will need depends on the amount of change you want to make, and the degree of smoothness you want between the frames. Start with a minimal set – the initial image, the end image and a couple of the stages in between. You can always add extra 'tween' images later.

Keep downloading times in mind! The animation file will be fractionally smaller than the sum of the individual files – half a dozen 5Kb GIFs (about 100 pixels square) will produce an animation of around 25Kb, which should download in under 10 seconds. With larger animations, you might want to let your visitors know what's coming and that it is worth waiting for!

Microsoft GIF Animator

One of the best (free) GIF animation programs around is Microsoft GIF Animator. Microsoft no longer supply it directly, but you should be able to track a copy down on the Web – at the time of writing, it can be downloaded from Softpile (at **http://www.softpile.com**).

Here's how to create an animated GIF.

1 Click the ![Open icon] **Open** button and select the first image.

2 Click the ![Insert icon] **Insert** button and select the next image. It will be inserted above the first – use ![down arrow icon] to move it down.

3 Insert and move the rest in the same way.

4 Switch to the **Animation** tab, turn on **Looping** and set the **Repeat Count** or turn on **Repeat Forever**.

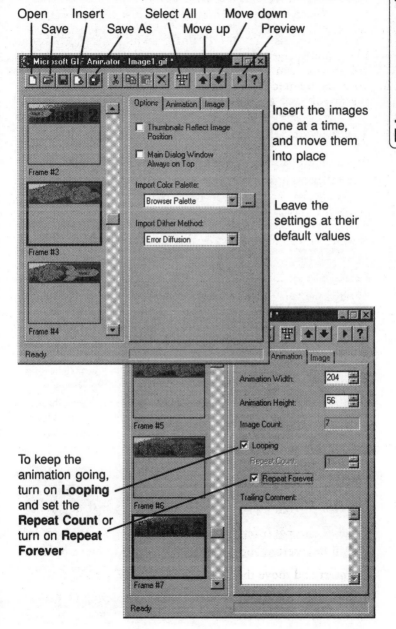

Open
Save
Insert
Save As
Select All
Move up
Move down
Preview

Insert the images
one at a time,
and move them
into place

Leave the
settings at their
default values

To keep the
animation going,
turn on **Looping**
and set the
Repeat Count or
turn on **Repeat
Forever**

5 Before you do anything else, save the file – there is a bug which can cause the program to crash at the next stage! Click the 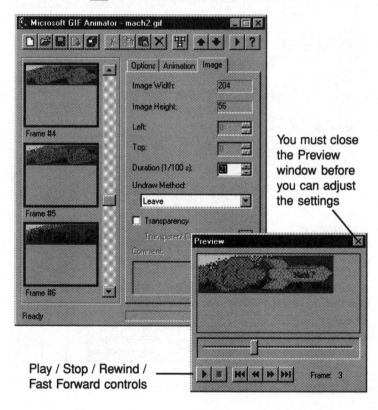 Save As button and give the file a name.

6 Switch to the **Image** tab.

7 If you want to set the same delay for all (or most) images, click the ⊞ **Select All** button, then set the **Duration**.

8 Otherwise, select each image in turn and set its **Duration**.

9 Click the ▶ **Preview** button and see how it looks. If necessary, close the Preview window and adjust the Durations to get the effect you want.

10 Click the ▣ **Save** button to save your changes.

You must close the Preview window before you can adjust the settings

Play / Stop / Rewind / Fast Forward controls

12.2 JavaScript

JavaScript is one of the easiest programming languages to learn – largely because you do not have to write complete programs to produce results! JavaScript code is written into the HTML documents, and is interpreted and executed by the browser.

The code may consist of a single instruction, attached to a button on a form, and activated by a click. For example:

```
<INPUT TYPE = button VALUE = "Click me"
   onClick = "alert('Hello visitor')">
```

When the button is clicked, the **onClick** event is picked up by the browser, which then runs the attached code. This opens an alert message box, carrying the greeting. The quotes in that line are crucial. The JavaScript code is enclosed in double quotes; the text of the message is enclosed in single quotes.

This idea is taken a little further in the next example, where the message box carries a greeting to the visitor. The code reads:

```
onClick = "alert('Hello ' + form1.visitor.value)"
```

This is used with a text box named 'visitor'. The code reads the contents of that box and adds it to 'Hello' to form a greeting.

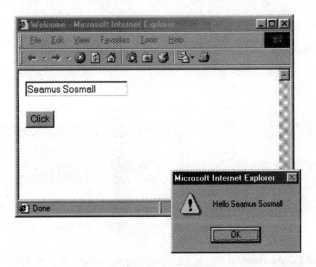

Simple responses to button clicks are easily done in JavaScript

Here's the complete code:

```
<HTML>
<HEAD>
<TITLE>Welcome</TITLE>
</HEAD>
<BODY>
<FORM NAME = form1>
<INPUT TYPE = text NAME = visitor VALUE = "Name
please">
<P><INPUT TYPE = button VALUE = "Click"
    onClick = "alert('Hello ' + form1.visitor.value)">
</FORM>
</BODY>
</HTML>
```

If you want to display a message in the Status line, you can do this from JavaScript. The expression takes the format:

```
self.status = "message"
```

self refers to the current window.

The code could be activated from a button click, or when the page is loaded. In the latter case, we attach to the **onLoad** event, which fits into the BODY tag. This gives us the line:

```
<BODY onLoad = "self.status = 'Welcome to my page' ">
```

Again, notice those quotes – double round the whole lot, and single quotes around text within the code.

Here's a working example, with a message appearing when the page loads, and a new one when the user clicks the button.

```
<HTML>
<BODY onLoad = "self.status = 'Welcome to my page' ">
<FORM>
<INPUT TYPE = button VALUE = "Going?"
    onClick = "self.status = 'Thanks for dropping by' ">
</FORM>
</BODY>
</HTML>
```

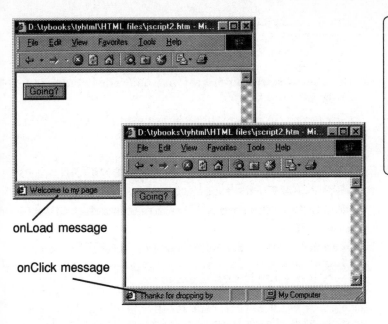

onLoad message

onClick message

These little examples demonstrate what you can do with just a couple of lines of JavaScript. There are lots of bigger examples around on the Internet – at the time of writing, there are a few in my JavaScript Sampler at **http://homepages.tcp.co.uk/ ~macbride** and I'll be writing more in 2003 to accompany my new book *Teach Yourself JavaScript*.

12.3 Java applets

Java applets are self-contained programs that run within Web pages. They are pulled into the page through the <APPLET> tag which specifies the applet code and sets the size of the display area. To cater for those users who cannot, or do not want to, view applets, alternative text or an image can be included. This example runs the *piano* applet in a 500 × 400 box, or displays the message if the browser cannot handle Java.

```
<APPLET CODE = "piano.class" WIDTH = 500 HEIGHT = 400>
   If you had Java you could play my piano!
</APPLET>
```

It is very satisfying to write your own applets, but learning Java properly is a major undertaking. You may prefer to make use of other people's efforts. The Internet has plenty of ready-written applets which you can adapt to suit your pages – though these tend to carry (prominent and undeletable) adverts for the original author's site.

Applets can be customized through the use of *parameters*. Values can be passed from HTML to the applet through <PARAM> tags.

```
<APPLET CODE = banner.class WIDTH = 500 HEIGHT = 200>
<PARAM NAME = message VALUE = "Welcome to my page">
<IMG SRC = welcome.gif ALT = "This page is better with Java">
</APPLET>
```

This applet has two parameters that let you set the message to be displayed. Notice how it caters for browsers that do not support Java – it will display an image, or text, if images are turned off. Ready-made applets that use parameters will also have the relevant HTML code for downloading. All you will need to do is change the text or numbers in the VALUE expressions.

Teach Yourself Java

If you want to learn Java, try Chris Wright's *Teach Yourself Java*, available where you bought this book.

Summary

◆ Animated GIFs catch the eye and are easily produced with software such as Microsoft's GIF Animator.

◆ JavaScript is not difficult to learn, and even small amounts of code can help to make a page more interactive.

◆ Java applets can be embedded in HTML pages. You can find ready-made ones on the Internet.

13

HTML summary

13.1 HTML tags and options

Structure

<HTML> </HTML> Enclose the whole document

<HEAD> </HEAD> Enclose the information area

<TITLE></TITLE> Define the name to appear in the title bar, and in browsers' favorites.

<META> Used to carry the author's name, search keywords and other information.

<ISINDEX> Defines phrases for keyword searches.

<BASE HREF = ...> Sets the base URL. Use it where files are stored in a set of folders and sub-folders.

<SCRIPT> Defines the scripting language, e.g. JavaScript, that is used on the page.

<APPLET ...> Defines a Java applet.

<STYLE TYPE = text/css> ... </STYLE> to enclose a style definition block in an HTML document.

...**TYPE = text/css STYLE =** *style definitions* ... can be used within most tags to define a style within the BODY.

<LINK REL=STYLESHEET TYPE=text/css HREF = url> to create a link to a .css style sheet file.

<BODY> </BODY> Enclose the displayed page.

> **BACKGROUND =** *Image*, repeated if space available
>
> **BGCOLOR =** *Colour value* of background
>
> **TEXT =** *Colour value* of text
>
> **LINK =** *Colour value* of unvisited links
>
> **VLINK =** *Colour value* of visited links
>
> **ALINK =** *Colour value* of active links.

<DIV ...> ... </DIV> encloses a set of elements within a page for styling. Styles can be defined directly within the <DIV> tag, or indirectly through a CLASS or ID option.

> **CLASS =** *classname* used within a tag to select a class definition for that tag.
>
> **ID =** *idname* also used within a tag to select a named definition for that tag.

<SPAN> ... </SPAN> as <DIV>, but enclosing an area within an element.

Headings and breaks

<Hn></Hn> Heading at level *n*: 1 is largest, 6 the smallest
<P> Start of Paragraph
   ALIGN = *Left/Center/Right* aligns text

  Line Break
<HR> Horizontal Rule
   SIZE = *Value* in pixels
   WIDTH = *Value* in pixels or percentage
   NOSHADE Makes the line solid
<PRE></PRE> Preformatted text; preserves line breaks
<ADDRESS></ADDRESS> Normally holds author's address
<!... comment ...> Not displayed by browser
<CENTER></CENTER> Centres text (or images)

Character formats

<B></B> **Bold**
<CITE></CITE> Citation – used for quotations
<CODE></CODE> Computer source code
<EM></EM> Emphasized = <I>
<FONT ...></FONT> Enclosed text to be formatted with one or more of these options:
   SIZE = *Number*, 1 to 7 (largest) for size of text
   COLOR = *Colour value* of following text
   FACE = *Font name* or family
<I></I> *Italic*
<KBD></KBD> Keyboard entry = <TT>
<SAMP></SAMP> Text sample
<STRONG></STRONG> Strongly emphasized = <B>
  Superscript
  Subscript
<TT></TT> `Typewriter`
<VAR></VAR> Variable name

Lists

<UL></UL> Unordered (bulleted) List
<OL></OL> Ordered (numbered or lettered) List
<LI> List Item
<DL></DL> Definition List
<DT> Term in definition list
<DD> Definition

Links and anchors

<A HREF = *URL>Link***</A>** Hypertext link between *Link* text
  or image and local or remote *URL*
<A NAME = *Target>Text***</A>** Creates a jump target in a page

Images

<IMG SRC = *Image>* Displays the *Image* (GIF or JPG)
  ALT = *Text* to display if image is not downloaded
  ALIGN = *Top/Bottom/Middle* aligns following text
  HEIGHT = *Value* in pixels or percentage of window height
  WIDTH = *Value* in pixels or percentage of window width

Forms

<FORM...></FORM> Encloses the Form area
  METHOD = *Post* (*Get*, not covered here, also possible)
  ACTION = Your e-mail address
<INPUT ...> Data entry by visitor
  NAME = *Name* of variable to store data
  SIZE = *Width* in characters
  TYPE = *Checkbox/Radio* options
      Reset/Submit/Button buttons
      Password hides input text
<TEXTAREA ...> Multi-line text entry
  NAME = *Name* of variable to store data
  ROWS = *Number* of rows to display
  COLS = *Number* of columns to display

<SELECT ...> Sets up a drop-down list

   NAME = *Name* of variable to store data

   SIZE = *Number* of items to display at one time

   MULTIPLE Allow multiple selections

<OPTION VALUE = *RetVal> ListItem* Display *ListItem* in Select list; pass *RetVal* to NAME variable

</SELECT> Closes Select list

Tables

<TABLE ...></TABLE> Encloses Table code

   BORDER = *Width* of border; narrow if no *width* given;

   CELLSPACING = *Value* in pixels of distance between inner and outer borders

   CELLPADDING = *Value* in pixels of distance between inner border and text

<CAPTION ...></CAPTION> Encloses text of caption

   ALIGN = *Top/Bottom* – default to *Top*

<TR></TR> Encloses a row

<TH ...></TH> Enclose a row or column header cell

<TD ...></TD> Enclose a data cell

   COLSPAN = *Number* of columns to spread cell across

   ROWSPAN = *Number* of rows to stretch cell down

   ALIGN = *Left/Right/Center* horizontal alignment of item in header or data cell

   VALIGN = *Top/Middle/Bottom* vertical alignment

   WIDTH = *Value* in pixels for width of cell

Frames

<FRAMESET ...> Start of frame section, in layout document and replacing the normal BODY elements. The tag must contain either a ROWS or COLS option.

   ROWS = Divides the window into frames horizontally, specifying the size of each either in pixels, or as a percentage of the space, or using '*' to share remaining space.

   COLS = Divides the window into frames vertically, specifying sizes as above.

</FRAMESET> End of frame section.

<FRAME ...> Defines the content and nature of a frame.

SRC = URL of document.

NAME = Name of frame, if to be used as TARGET of HREF link.

SCROLLING = *Yes/No/Auto* – controls appearance of scroll bars around frame.

NORESIZE Forces fixed size frame.

<NOFRAMES></NOFRAMES> Encloses code to be displayed in browsers which cannot handle frames.

TARGET = *Name/Self/Parent/Top/Blank* – HREF option to specify where a document is to be displayed.

13.2 Style sheets

Attributes and settings

Keywords used for settings are shown in *italics*.

Sizes can be given in units of em (size of letter 'm'), cm or px (pixels), unless otherwise stated.

Colours can be given as names or by *rgb(red_val, green_val, blue_val)* where values are numbers in the range 0 to 255.

The *none* setting is used to turn off settings that may have been inherited from a parent element or earlier definition of an element.

Font

font-family: font names (in "quotes" if they contain spaces) with a generic name as last alternative. The generic names are *serif, sans-serif, cursive, fantasy, monospace.*

font-style: *normal, italic* or *oblique.*

font-variant: *normal* or *small-caps.*

font-weight: *lighter, normal, bold, bolder* or a value 100, 200 … 900.

font-size: *xx-small, x-small, small, medium, large, x-large, xx-large, larger, smaller*, a percentage or size in points (*pt*).

font: list of values for all or some of font-style, font-variant, font-weight, font-size and font-family.

color: colour_value.

Background

background-color: colour_value or *transparent.*

background-image: *url* (hyperlink or filename) or *none.*

background-repeat: *repeat, repeat-x, repeat-y* or *no-repeat.*

background-attachment: *scroll* or *fixed.*

background-position: distance from top and left as percentage or size; or keywords *top, center* or *bottom, left, center* or *right.*

background: list of values for background-color; background-image; background-repeat; background-attachment; background-position.

Text properties

word-spacing: *normal* or value in ems.

letter-spacing: *normal* or value in ems.

text-align: *left*, *right*, *center* or *justify*.

vertical-align: *baseline*, *sub*, *super*, *text-top*, *middle*, *text-bottom*, sets alignment relative to the parent element – could be used to pick out a word in a paragraph.

text-indent: *value* in ems, cm or px, or as a percentage of the window.

line-height: *normal* or size, or as a percentage of the font size. Sets the distance between lines of text in a paragraph.

text-decoration: *none*, *underline*, *overline*, *line-through* or *blink*.

text-transform: *capitalize* (initial), *uppercase*, *lowercase*, *none* (used to cancel setting inherited from parent element or style sheet).

Box properties

These control the size, position and borders of elements.

width: size, percentage of window or *auto*.

height: size, percentage of window or *auto*.

float: *left*, *right* or *none*.

clear: *none*, *left*, *right* or *both*.

margin: sets all the margins at once. If one size is given, it is applied to all sides. If four are given, they are read as top, right, bottom and left. If there are two or three, the missing values are taken from the opposite side.

margin-top, **margin-right**, **margin-bottom**, **margin-left**: size, percentage of window or *auto*. Sets each margin separately.

padding: sets all four at once, as **margin**.

padding-top, **padding-right**, **padding-bottom**, **padding-left**: size, or percentage of window. Sets each padding separately.

border-width: sets all border widths at once. As margin except that if two sizes are given, top and bottom widths are set to the first, right and left are set to the second.

border-top-width, **border-right-width**, **border-bottom-width**, **border-left-width**: *thin*, *medium*, *thick* or size. Sets each width separately.

border-color: from one to four colour names or values, applied to the sides as for **border-width**.

border-style: one to four of *none, dotted, dashed, solid, double, groove, ridge, inset, outset,* applied to the sides as for **border-width** above.

border: up to three values to set border-width, border-style and color for all four sides at once.

Lists

list-style-type: *disc, circle, square, decimal, lower-roman, upper-roman, lower-alpha, upper-alpha* or *none.*

Combines the UL and OL TYPE options for the <LI> tag.

list-style-image: *url(hyperlink or filename)* or *none.* Sets an image as the bullet for a list item.

list-style-position: *inside* or *outside.* Sets the position of the bullet in relation to the list item.

Miscellaneous

display: *block, inline, list-item or none* (turns off the display of the element).

Elements fall naturally into three categories: block, e.g. P, H1 and IMG; inline, e.g. B and I; and list-item, LI. They can be redefined into another category – though you would need a convincing reason to mess with this!

white-space: *normal, pre* (as <PRE> tag) or *nowrap.*

A:link, A:visited, A:active colour_value.

These are 'pseudo-classes' used to set alternative colours for the anchor tag.

14

taking it further

14.1 The start not the end

This book was never intended to be a complete course in HTML, but it has, I hoped, given you a good grounding in all aspects of HTML and helped you to develop the confidence to go on further.

So where do you go from here? There are two main routes of development. The first comes from within you. Master what you have learnt so far and bring your creativity to bear. Play with the building bricks of HTML and see what you can construct with them. What do you want to say, and how can you say it with what you already know? The second route looks beyond. What other tools, techniques and languages are available to the Web page developer? What are other people doing? What can you learn from more experienced page builders?

There are plenty of books around on HTML and Web page development, including three in the *Teach Yourself* series: *Java*, *JavaScript* and *E-Commerce*. There is also lots of information, samples and services for Web developers available on the Web. Here are just a few selected sites.

14.2 Web sites for Web developers

The HTML Working Group

http://www.w3.org/MarkUp

These are the people who are responsible for HTML – the ones who set the standards and define how the code works. Amongst other things, you will find the full specification for the latest version of HTML (http://www.w3.org/TR/html401/). You might also like to read about XHTML, Extensible HyperText Markup Language, which looks likely to replace HTML in the long term.

HTML Writers Guild

http://www.hwg.org/

This is one of the leading educational organizations for Web developers, with over 150,000 members around the world. It offers many training courses, plus other facilities including a regular newsletter to help keep you up to date.

DevEdge

http://devedge.netscape.com/

The main Netscape-based site for Web developers. Though Internet Explorer is far and away the leading browser, there are still a lot of people who use Netscape – about 20% of regular Internet users. If you want to make sure that they can see your pages properly, it's worth checking out the Netscape variations.

AddMe

http://www.addme.com

The one-stop approach to advertising your page.

Babel

http://www.geocities.com/ikind_babel/babel/babel.html

Glossary of Internet acronyms and abbreviations.

Google

http://www.google.com

Whatever you are looking for, if it is on the Web, you can find it through Google.

Java Boutique

http://javaboutique.internet.com/

This is *the* place to start to explore Java.

The JavaScript Source

http://javascript.internet.com/

And this is the place to start to explore JavaScript.

MapEdit

http://www.boutell.com/index.html

Software for easy image map creation.

Microsoft Developer Network

http://msdn.microsoft.com/library

A major reference source for HTML and many programming languages. Follow the links through *HTML and Dynamic HTML* to *Reference* then *HTML Elements*.

Shareware Central

http://www.shareware.com

An excellent place to find shareware.

Web Monkey

http://hotwired.lycos.com/webmonkey/

A great resource for developers, packed with ideas, help and advice, plus stacks of animations and ready-made Java and JavaScript routines, that can be added to your pages.

Web Tools

http://www.webtools.org/counter

Go here to add a counter to your page

Yahoo

http://www.yahoo.com

The best of the Internet directories – you can find almost everything from here.

Newsgroups

If you want to swap ideas with other enthusiasts, try the newsgroups. There are over 60 on aspects of HTML, over 70 for Java programmers and a dozen on JavaScript.

index